بسم الله الرحمن الرحيم

The Chains Did Not Win

Omar ibn Said

The Chains Did Not Win, *Omar ibn Said*
By: Gus Kazem   12/28/2025

First Edition.
ISBN: 979-8-90280-011-8

Gusgraph

www.Gusgraph.com

Dedication

This book is for those whose names were carried farther than their bodies, whose lives were interrupted but not erased. For those who learned that silence can be a form of survival, and memory a form of prayer. For the ones who endured without witnesses, who practiced faith without permission, who kept order alive inside themselves when the world around them abandoned it. It is for those who were owned but not possessed, counted but not comprehended, renamed but never fully rewritten. And it is for the truth that waited patiently, knowing that one day, even late, even with trembling hands, it would be placed into the world and remain.

Gus Kazem,

Disclaimer

This work is rooted in the surviving writings of Omar ibn Said and in the historical record surrounding his life. Where the record falls silent, narrative continuity has been shaped with care, restraint, and fidelity to the world he inhabited. This book does not claim to replace history, but to listen closely to it — and to what it could not fully preserve.

The spiritual language used here reflects the shared inheritance of those who speak to the Divine across traditions. Terms have been rendered for universal understanding, without altering the substance of the faith Omar carried and practiced in captivity.

Scenes of enslavement are presented as they were lived: without spectacle, without mitigation. Nothing here is intended to soften the reality of bondage or to reconcile it with the language of mercy. Any dignity that appears belongs to the enduring human spirit, not to the systems that sought to own it.

This book asks the reader not for agreement, but for attention.

Preface

In the name of God, the Compassionate, the Sustainer of all that breathes and endures. All praise belongs to Him alone, Lord of the seen and the unseen, the One before whom every beginning and every ending must eventually stand. To Him belongs judgment, mercy, and the ordering of time beyond human measure.

O God, You are the light that remains when all other lights are taken. From the depth of frailty and remembrance, this work is placed before You. Words bend under their own weight when they approach what You have allowed to endure. Yet even faltering speech is an offering when it is given with care. Accept what is incomplete, and make what is truthful sufficient.

This book rises from a life carried farther than it was ever meant to go.

It is the account of a man formed in discipline, memory, and devotion, who crossed an ocean not by choice but by force, and lived long enough within captivity to leave a record behind. Omar ibn Said did not arrive in the Americas seeking witness. He was taken there, unnamed by the systems that claimed him, misread by the language that surrounded him, and measured by standards that could not comprehend what he carried.

What survived him is brief. What surrounds it is vast.

This book does not attempt to enlarge his voice beyond recognition, nor to smooth the fractures left by enslavement into narrative comfort. It listens closely to what remains, and where the record falls silent, it moves with restraint. What is imagined here is shaped by historical ground, by the limits imposed upon his life, and by the discipline evident in the words he chose to leave behind.

Omar lived among people who prayed, yet could not hear him fully. He practiced faith where faith was not permitted its own name. He carried a Divine Scripture in memory, one that spoke in continuity with earlier revelations, close enough to be mistaken for familiarity, distant enough to remain unseen. His endurance was not loud. It did not argue. It persisted.

This book does not ask the reader to admire suffering or to reconcile it with mercy. It does not offer captivity as instruction or endurance as consolation. It records what was lived without spectacle, what was preserved without permission, and what was written when the body could no longer carry memory alone.

What appears in these pages is not perfection untouched by trial, but fidelity maintained within it.

History often preserves the structures that dominate and forgets the inner lives that resisted erasure without force. This work attends to one such life, not to complete it, but to honor its continuity. What Omar ibn Said left behind is not a closed testimony. It is a hand extended across time, offering alignment rather than explanation.

This book asks not for agreement, but for attention.

الله

Gus Kazem is a spiritual storyteller and researcher devoted to lives shaped under pressure, where faith endured without guarantee and meaning was carried quietly across loss. His work moves between historical record and inward remembrance, seeking clarity without intrusion and depth without distortion.

In this book, he traces the life of Omar ibn Said with restraint and care, allowing silence to retain its authority and endurance to speak without embellishment. When not writing, Gus continues his work in healing, study, and service, attentive to the unseen continuities that bind memory, faith, and responsibility across generations.

When not writing, Gus continues his work in Ruqyah, spiritual healing, community service, and silent contemplation beneath starlit skies.

Contents

Dedication..IV

Disclaimer V

Preface VI

Introduction X

Author's Note XIII

Historical Note..XV

Chapter: 1 The Horizon 1

Chapter: 2 Taken 14

Chapter: 3 The Ocean 24

Chapter: 4 Unread Country 35

Chapter: 5 Flight 50

Chapter: 6 The Jail...59

Chapter: 7 Owned House 69

Chapter: 8 Faith in Captivity....................................81

Chapter: 9 Borrowed Time.......................................91

Chapter: 10 Final Writing...100

Timeline..108

Sources & Acknowledgments.................................109

Image Credits..110

Introduction

This is a book about a journey.
Not the kind traced across maps or measured by miles, but a journey forced upon a man whose life was already ordered, whose direction had already been set. A journey carved into the body rather than chosen by the will. A passage that began not with departure, but with rupture, and continued across land and water long after choice had been stripped away.

It is a book about distance that does not end when movement stops.

About roads that erase as they carry. About an ocean that does not separate one shore from another so much as it rearranges everything a man thought he knew about time, memory, and survival. It is about confinement that follows motion, and motion that continues even when the body is held still.

It is about a man formed in discipline before the world broke him open.

A man raised among prayer and study, shaped by sacred order, whose life was interrupted and carried elsewhere without consent. A man who crossed into a country that could not read him, could not hear his language clearly, could not recognize the scripture he carried inwardly, and yet depended on his endurance all the same.

This is not a book of heroic escape or simple triumph.

It does not smooth captivity into metaphor or turn survival into spectacle. What appears in these pages is lived reality, sustained without guarantee, recorded with restraint. History here is not polished. It is held together carefully, the way one holds something fragile that must still be carried forward.

It is a book about faith practiced without permission.

About devotion reduced to memory when posture was denied. About sacred words preserved inwardly when speaking them aloud invited danger. About resemblance mistaken for surrender, and silence mistaken for absence. About the quiet labor of remaining aligned in a world that had no use for alignment.

It is about a scripture carried without pages.

About words guarded through repetition when books were impossible. About remembrance treated not as comfort, but as responsibility. About memory becoming the last territory that could not be owned.

This book does not seek to resolve contradiction.

It holds them. Mercy beside bondage. Kindness beside possession. Growth beside erasure. Gratitude beside truth. It allows these to stand without forcing them into a single explanation, because the life at its center did not offer one.

And it is about writing.

About the moment when endurance gives way to witness. When a man whose body has belonged to others places part of himself beyond ownership, not through defiance, but through record. What is written here is not everything that was lived. It is what remained intact long enough to be placed on the page.
This is not a story preserved for admiration.
It is preserved for attention.

Because the journey traced here did not end with its subject. It echoes wherever lives are interrupted, wherever faith is practiced inwardly because it cannot be practiced openly, wherever memory is asked to do the work of survival.

If you read these pages in quiet hours or crowded ones, know this: the journey does not ask you to become someone else. It asks you to recognize continuity. To see how a life carried under pressure can still retain order, and how witness, even late, even incomplete, can still stand.

Turn the page.
What follows is not a map.

It is a passage left behind by a man who crossed the world without leaving himself behind.

Author's Note

This book was not written from distance or ease. It emerged slowly, from years spent listening rather than declaring, from long hours attending to what history records briefly and what silence carries fully. It was shaped by patience more than confidence, by restraint more than certainty, and by a sustained effort to remain faithful to a life that did not ask to be explained, only to be understood carefully.

I did not approach this work as a scholar assembling conclusions, nor as a storyteller seeking ornament. I approached it as a witness to continuity. What survives of Omar ibn Said's life is fragile, partial, and burdened by the conditions that sought to erase him. Writing this book required accepting those limits without attempting to correct them through invention or excess. Where the record speaks, I listened. Where it falls silent, I moved slowly, guided by history, context, and the discipline evident in the man himself.

This is not a book about abstraction.

It is about faith lived under pressure, carried inwardly when expression was denied, preserved through memory when practice was constrained. It is about endurance that did not announce itself, and devotion that remained intact without needing permission or recognition. The life traced here reminds us that faith is not proven through display, but through fidelity maintained when no witness is present.

If clarity appears in these pages, it belongs to the truth that endured long enough to be written. If coherence holds, it is because the life at the center of this book was shaped by order long before it was broken by force. If there are faults here, they are mine, born of limitation rather than intent, and they are offered with humility rather than defense.

This book does not ask the reader to admire suffering or to reconcile injustice with mercy. It asks only for attention. To see how a life constrained almost entirely by others could still retain allegiance to something higher. To recognize that continuity does not always arrive through triumph, but sometimes through quiet persistence carried to the end.

If these pages leave you more attentive to lives history compresses into margins, if they sharpen your awareness of what faith can look like when stripped of comfort and voice, then the work has served its purpose.

What follows is not a conclusion.

It is a record placed carefully into the world, entrusted to the reader without instruction on what must be done with it. Like the life it traces, it asks only to be carried forward with care.

Gus Kazem,
The Author

Historical Note

The life of Omar ibn Said reaches us through fragments shaped by survival. His own writing, composed late in life in a language no longer permitted him freely, stands as the central record from which this work proceeds. It is brief, restrained, and marked by apology rather than assertion, written by a man conscious of failing strength and imperfect recall, yet careful to preserve order where he still could.

This book is grounded in that record.

Where Omar ibn Said speaks, his words are treated as anchor. Where history confirms circumstance, it is followed closely. Where silence remains, it is not filled hastily. Narrative continuity has been shaped with restraint, guided by historical context, cultural practice, and the discipline evident in Omar's own voice. No interior life has been invented to soften captivity or heighten drama. What is imagined here serves coherence, not consolation.

Omar ibn Said was born in West Africa, educated within a long-standing tradition of sacred learning, and taken by force into transatlantic enslavement in the early nineteenth century. He lived much of his life in the American South, passing through systems of ownership, imprisonment, and misinterpretation before leaving behind a handwritten Arabic manuscript that survives today. That document does not offer a full account of his life. It does not seek sympathy. It records fact, faith, and endurance without ornament.

This work does not attempt to reconcile contradiction or to resolve injustice through narrative framing. Enslavement is presented as it functioned: as a system that stripped agency while relying upon the very lives it constrained. Any dignity that appears belongs to the human spirit that endured within that system, not to the system itself.

Spiritual language throughout this book has been rendered in universal terms to reflect continuity across revealed traditions while remaining faithful to the substance of Omar ibn Said's devotion. Scripture is not cited to instruct, but to situate memory where memory itself became an act of worship.

This book is not a replacement for history, nor an expansion of Omar ibn Said's voice beyond recognition. It is an act of listening across time, shaped by what remains and by what was never allowed to be fully preserved. Where certainty ends, care begins.

What follows should be read not as completion, but as continuation: a life carried forward as faithfully as the record allows, without excess, without reduction, and without claiming authority that does not belong to it.

Chapter: 1 The Horizon

Capture does not begin with chains, but with the sudden removal of choice.

Quote:

"They were taken by force, and the world shifted without asking."

The Land That Knew His Name

Before the ocean entered his life, Before the ocean entered his life, before iron learned the measure of his wrists, there was a land that knew him by placement rather than announcement, where a man's name was spoken with an understanding of who had taught him, who had raised him, and what obligations governed his days. That land lay between waters, stretched along a river that moved steadily and without urgency, feeding narrow fields and binding memory to soil, a place where the earth was not generous but dependable, and dependability was valued more than abundance. Faith there was not inward or abstract; it was structural, embedded into time, movement, and speech. He was born into order, not comfort, but a system that did not bend to impulse. Days began before light, when washing followed sequence and purpose rather than refreshment, and readiness mattered more than ease. Time was divided and claimed in advance by duty.

Words were learned slowly and guarded once learned because language carried consequence; accuracy preserved meaning, and error could fracture lives. He spent years in study that did not present themselves as heroic, years of listening, repetition, correction, and memorization, seated among others under teachers who corrected far more than they praised, shaping him through refusal rather than encouragement.

Theology was not speculation but orientation, law not dominance but restraint, grammar not ornament but protection, memory not nostalgia but survival. Faith did not hover above existence in that land; it governed it. Prayer fixed the day into immovable points, giving fixed wealth into obligation, and movement toward sacred places into devotion. Nothing was optional, nothing symbolic. Preparation was not questioned because it was the cost of remaining intact in a world that expected discipline.

Image: 1 Riding through the savanna on a donkey

When he returned home after those years, he returned formed, not finished but settled into a rhythm that required no approvalHis prayers followed the sun, his giving followed the harvest, and his days passed without remark, because meaning functioned quietly and reliably. The land received him because it had shaped him, holding the trace of his movement without resistance.

There was no sense of departure yet, no warning sharp enough to disturb the assumption that order was permanent and older than threat. Then the horizon changed without gradual warning. Men arrived who did not recognize lineage or instruction. Fire replaced teaching. Command replaced obligation. The land that had known his name could not defend it. In that single rupture, the rhythm governing his life tore open, and the silence that followed was not peace but vacancy.

MAURITANIA

Senegal River

B

SENEGAL

M

Manant
dam

GAMBIA

GUINEA
BISSAU

GUINEA

Everything that would later be taken from him began there,
at the moment when order failed and did not return.

His prayers followed the sun, his giving followed the
harvest, and his days passed without remark, because
meaning functioned quietly and reliably. The land received
him because it had shaped him, holding the trace of his
movement without resistance. There was no sense of
departure yet, no warning sharp enough to disturb the
assumption that order was permanent and older than
threat.

Then the horizon changed without gradual warning. Men
arrived who did not recognize lineage or instruction. Fire
replaced teaching. Command replaced obligation. The land
that had known his name could not defend it. In that single
rupture, the rhythm governing his life tore open, and the
silence that followed was not peace but vacancy.
Everything that would later be taken from him began there,
at the moment when order failed and did not return.

Image: 2 Omar ibn Said's Handwriting
(Opening Page)

The hand is careful, disciplined, already conscious of
its own limits. These are not decorative marks. They
are a life trained to order, placing itself onto the page
with restraint, apology, and resolve.

A Life Shaped by Discipline

Discipline did not enter his life as a decision or a philosophy; it was present before preference formed, before the body learned it could resist, built into the hours so completely that deviation would have felt like disorder rather than freedom.

He rose before light because the day required alignment before it could be entered, and water met skin in a fixed sequence learned so early it felt older than conscious memory, not for comfort or refreshment but to prepare the body to stand correctly within an ordered world.

The body was trained first, through repetition and restraint, and the mind followed after, shaped by years that passed without spectacle or interruption. He sat longer than most men could endure sitting, listening through correction that did not soften itself for pride or fatigue, learning words slowly and deliberately, testing them through repetition until they could be trusted to hold under pressure.

Theology did not offer reassurance; it provided orientation. Law did not elevate; it restricted. Grammar was approached as a safeguard against error, learned with the seriousness of a tool that, if misused, could cause harm.

Memory was trained until it could carry weight steadily, because what was retained mattered as much as what was spoken.

Image: 3 Islamic school in Senegal's evening light

His teachers were present and exacting, not distant figures preserved by reverence, but men who corrected immediately and without apology, treating error not as expression but as risk, because in their understanding the world punished imprecision more harshly than any classroom ever would. Discipline was not gentle, but it was deliberate, rooted in the assumption that endurance was a necessary skill rather than a virtue to be admired.

Faith did not sit above his life as ornament or abstraction; it structured it. Prayer divided the day into fixed points that did not yield to mood, weather, or weariness. Giving was not generosity in sentiment but accounting in practice, an acknowledgment that what passed through his hands was not fully his to keep.

Movement toward sacred places was not romanticized; distance itself was part of the obligation, and cost was integral to meaning. Nothing functioned as symbol alone. Everything served a purpose. This shaping did not produce softness or ease; it produced endurance.

A man formed this way does not unravel when routine falters; he holds inward order while waiting for structure to reassert itself. He learns to guard speech not because silence is admired, but because words carry consequence. He learns to maintain internal discipline even when the outer world becomes uncertain. When discipline is complete, it becomes invisible. It feels like normalcy.

It feels permanent. It persuades a man that the world, however severe, still operates by intelligible rules. Here, before any rupture, discipline was not a defense or preparation for catastrophe; it was simply life, lived without question, in a world that still recognized order and returned stability to those who submitted to it fully.

Image: 4 Manuscript Page with Autobiographical Lines

The life appears briefly, without ornament.
Education, capture, and removal are named
without explanation. Silence surrounds the facts,
not because they were small, but because
endurance does not need emphasis.

The Day Order Collapsed

Order did not end through debate or gradual neglect; it ended abruptly, the way a structure fails when struck with sufficient force at a vulnerable point, functioning fully in one moment and collapsing in the next without warning. Men arrived carrying violence rather than obligation, speaking not to be answered but to move bodies, and what had once been governed by instruction and correction was overtaken by command and fire.

The land that had recorded lineage, discipline, and responsibility with the steadiness of a ledger was torn open by voices that recognized none of it, leaving no council to appeal to and no law that could be recited with expectation of effect. Authority dissolved in the presence of force, and with it disappeared the assumption that the world, however demanding, still operated according to knowable rules.

He did not preserve details of faces or banners or numbers, recording only that a large army came, that many men were killed, and that he was taken, a restraint that reflects the nature of the moment itself, which did not allow reflection or interpretation but erased both. The discipline that had once governed his days did not vanish, but it lost its external anchors all at once, because ritual depends on space and time, and both were removed without transition.

Capture unfolded as sequence rather than instant: first the loss of authority, when elders could no longer intervene and teachers could no longer correct; then the loss of rhythm, when prayer could not be observed at its appointed times and washing became impractical; then the loss of choice, when movement ceased to belong to him and speech lost relevance.

Image: 5 European raiders assault West African village

His body was handled as though already categorized, while the mind struggled to absorb a reality that no longer corresponded to anything it had been trained to expect. The road away from home opened without ceremony, and each forced step forward converted distance into something permanent, the familiar landscape receding not with drama but with efficiency, overtaken by dust, urgency, and the press of movement. There was no opportunity to gather meaning or assign significance; whatever meaning survived would have to do so without structure or reinforcement.

This was the point at which order truly collapsed, not at the sound of killing itself but when time ceased to behave as it always had, when morning no longer announced itself with clarity and night did not close the day cleanly, and effort replaced sequence as days blurred into unmarked exertion.

The internal discipline remained intact, but it no longer aligned with the external world, creating a dissonance that could not be resolved through habit alone.

He did not record resistance or prayer during this passage; he recorded outcome, a choice that reflects discipline stripped to its core, focused on observation and retention when expression no longer altered circumstance.

When reason fails to shape events, a man trained in order learns to conserve what remains by moving, watching, and remembering rather than reacting.

The horizon that once represented continuity became a boundary of separation, beyond which waited an expanse of water he had never seen and a crossing he had no framework to imagine, a future that would not recognize the form he had been shaped into.

The collapse was complete not because life ended, but because the world he understood ended, and from that point forward, order would no longer be provided by place or structure but would have to be carried inwardly across a landscape determined to strip it away.

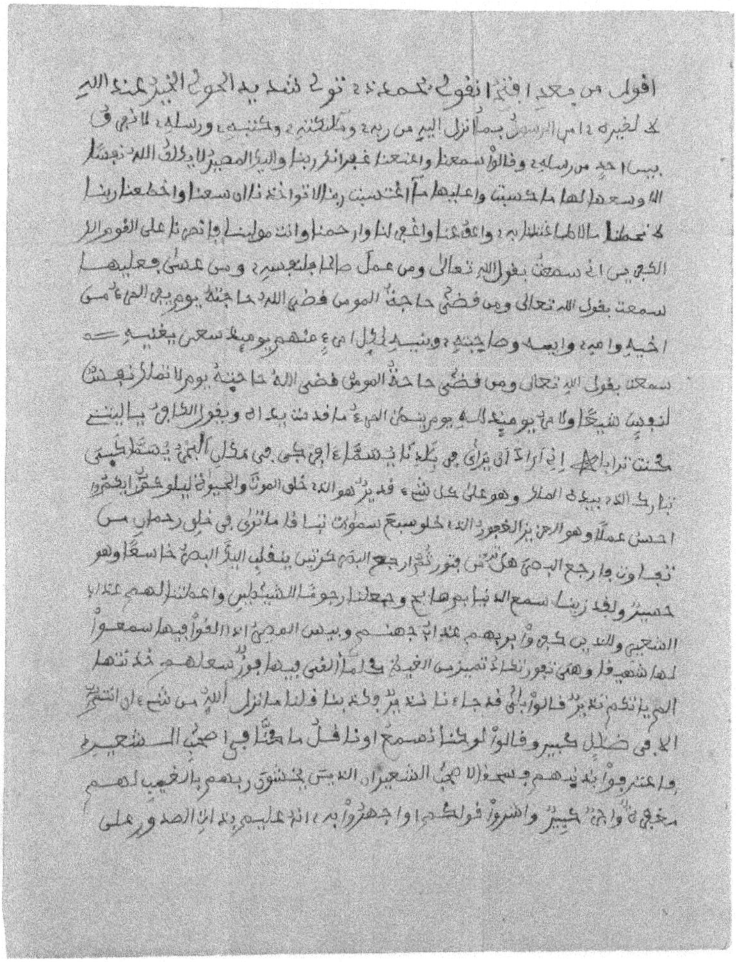

Image: 6 Manuscript Page with Autobiographical Lines

The life appears briefly, without ornament. Education, capture, and removal are named without explanation. Silence surrounds the facts, not because they were small, but because endurance does not need emphasis.

Chapter: 2 Taken

Capture does not begin with chains, but with the sudden removal of choice.

Quote:

"They were taken by force, and the world shifted without asking."

The Army Without Faces

They did not arrive as individuals but as function, a body of men moved by command rather than character and defined by result rather than motive, and Omar never names them or marks them with symbols because naming would imply presence and presence would imply meaning, neither of which was required.

They came to take, and violence preceded explanation because explanation was unnecessary; men fell not because they were selected but because they stood where force passed through, and death occurred without ceremony or pause, stripped of language that might slow the work. Elders spoke and were ignored, teachers stood and were passed by, and whatever authority had structured the land dissolved the moment it encountered violence that carried no consequence for refusal.

Omar was seized among others and bound without distinction, his hands, trained to hold and preserve sacred words, treated no differently than hands shaped by labor, because education did not register and lineage did not translate; only the capacity of a body to be moved mattered, everything else deferred or discarded. The taking was not chaotic but methodical, men organized the way cargo is organized, close enough to control and spaced enough to prevent unity, silence enforced not by instruction but by visible outcome, as those who questioned were corrected publicly and those who resisted were removed without ceremony, the line closing behind them as if absence required no accounting.

The land receded without farewell or ritual, not announced as loss but rendered unreachable through accumulation of distance, each forced step forward denying return and confirming that what had existed before now survived only in memory. Prayer times slipped beyond reach, washing became impossible, and speech turned into liability rather than expression, while the body learned a new obedience not to rhythm or devotion but to imposed direction.

Image: 7 Burning of a village in Africa, nineteenth century

A period engraving recording forced capture through destruction. Such images document rupture and method, not the full life that existed before it

Omar does not record fear or rage in this passage; he records movement, because movement is where condition replaces event, where it becomes clear that what has begun will not correct itself. The army did not pause to negotiate meaning or acknowledge consequence; it moved toward outcome, toward the coast, toward the great water he had never

seen, which would soon be known not through sight or description but through endurance. The army without faces carried no obligation to remember those it took, and that burden passed entirely to the taken, who carried memory forward in compressed and guarded form as the world that had shaped them disappeared behind dust, distance, and the certainty that nothing ahead would require their consent.

The Road to the Great Water

The road did not present itself as exile or transition; it asserted itself as movement that could not be refused, men pressed into lines and taught the pace through force rather than instruction, their bodies learning compliance before the mind could question it. The ground changed steadily beneath their feet, soil giving way to dust, stone cutting through weakened soles as the sun rose and fell without regard for what it exposed or concealed.

There was no place to stop long enough for the body to recover its sense of measure, and distance accumulated relentlessly, like hunger, until it eclipsed all other concerns.

He walked because walking was required, not toward anything he could name, but away from everything that had once provided structure. The land stretched outward, unfamiliar and indifferent, villages appearing briefly at the edge of vision and disappearing without invitation or pause. Water was distributed according to the needs of the march, not the demands of the body, and food arrived as calculation rather than nourishment, just enough to sustain movement. The line advanced whether men were ready or not, and readiness ceased to carry meaning.

Time lost its shape first; morning no longer announced obligation, and night no longer offered rest. Prayer could not be marked by posture or direction and folded inward, compressed into memory and repeated without sound, while washing became impossible and the body accumulated its own residue until discomfort faded into constant sensation. The discipline that had once ordered his life did not dissolve, but it withdrew, suspended without the conditions required to express itself.

Image: 8 A coffle moving inland, bodies bound into a single line, where distance erased names and the road itself became the first lesson in loss.

Language followed time into collapse; words spoken in his tongue found no recognition, and the words spoken around him were not meant to be understood but obeyed, making silence safer than precision and attention a liability.

He learned to look without engaging and to listen without response, reducing his presence to its minimum expression.

The road taught captivity before iron was applied, revealing that endurance is not dramatic but repetitive, sustained through refusal to collapse when collapse would simplify matters for those who controlled the line. It demonstrated that the body can be carried farther than belief anticipates and that belief, once broken, does not readily reform.

At night, fires burned at intervals sufficient to maintain control but insufficient to offer comfort, and sleep came in shallow fragments, the living adjusting themselves around the exhausted until distinction blurred.

Those unable to maintain pace did not slow the movement; the line closed and advanced without acknowledgment.

The great water was not yet visible, but its presence was already exerting force, pulling the road toward itself with certainty.

Counting increased, control tightened, and silence deepened as the land flattened and the air shifted, salt entering breath before the horizon revealed its source.

By the time the sea appeared, it arrived not as spectacle or wonder but as confirmation, the inevitable end toward which the road had been leading all along, stripping away what could not cross and preparing bodies for a passage that would demand obedience, silence, and survival without expectation.

The road ended at the water, and nothing he had been allowed to retain remained unaffected by that approach.

What Is Lost Before Chains

What is taken before chains is not metal or weight but structure, and that removal begins long before restraint becomes visible. During the march inland toward the coast, captivity establishes itself through sequence rather than spectacle, stripping away the systems that once allowed a man to locate himself in the world.

The first loss is time as order. Hours still pass, but they no longer carry meaning. Morning does not announce obligation, and night does not offer rest. Rising and stopping occur by command rather than rhythm, and the sun no longer governs the day. For a man trained to live inside measured intervals, this collapse is immediate and disorienting. Prayer cannot claim its appointed place because place itself has been taken, and direction has been replaced by enforced movement.

Time flattens into duration without markers, and discipline, which once aligned the body with expectation, is left without surface to press against. The next loss is language, not the ability to speak but the usefulness of speech. Words spoken in his own tongue are not received, and words spoken around him are not meant to communicate understanding but to produce movement. Commands are brief and unambiguous, shaped to be obeyed rather than interpreted. Language becomes risk rather than tool, and silence proves safer than precision.

Thought withdraws inward, where it can still be ordered and retained without interruption. This withdrawal is not surrender but conservation, a narrowing of exposure in response to conditions where expression produces no benefit. Status follows. In the land that shaped him, knowledge carried consequence, age commanded attention, and lineage established position.

On the road, none of this translates. Bodies are assessed only for endurance and capacity to move. Learning does not increase value unless it interferes with obedience, in which case it becomes liability.

Distinctions collapse into uniformity, and a life shaped by discipline is reduced to function. This reduction is not chaotic but systematic, applied consistently as the line advances. Then comes a loss that is difficult to define because it arrives without announcement: the loss of being addressed as someone whose presence matters. No one asks his name. No one waits for response.

Decisions occur around him without reference to his consent, and his body is handled as if permission has already been removed from consideration. Identity collapses into management. He is no longer seen, only positioned. This change completes the internal transition from person to unit, a transition enforced not through declaration but through repetition.

The road reinforces these losses daily. Movement continues regardless of fatigue. Food and water are distributed according to calculation rather than need. Those who cannot keep pace are not negotiated with; they are removed, and the line closes without pause.

Night offers little relief. Fires are set far enough apart to maintain control but close enough to prevent escape, and sleep comes in fragments shaped by cold ground and proximity to others equally exhausted.

The distinction between the living and the failing blurs, and endurance becomes collective by necessity rather than choice. Counting increases as the coast approaches. Control tightens. Silence deepens.

By the time the air changes and the land flattens, the road has completed its instruction. When iron finally appears, it does not introduce captivity but confirms what has already been established.

Chains formalize a condition that movement, deprivation, and erasure have enforced over time. They announce ownership after the fact.

What has been taken before chains cannot be restored by their removal. The loss of ordered time, of usable language, of recognized status, and of being addressed as someone whose presence carries weight must be rebuilt internally, without witness or acknowledgment.

By the time the ocean comes into view, the body has already been trained for passage, and the self has learned to survive without expectation.

The road ends at the water, but its work continues, because everything demanded next has already been rehearsed through loss.

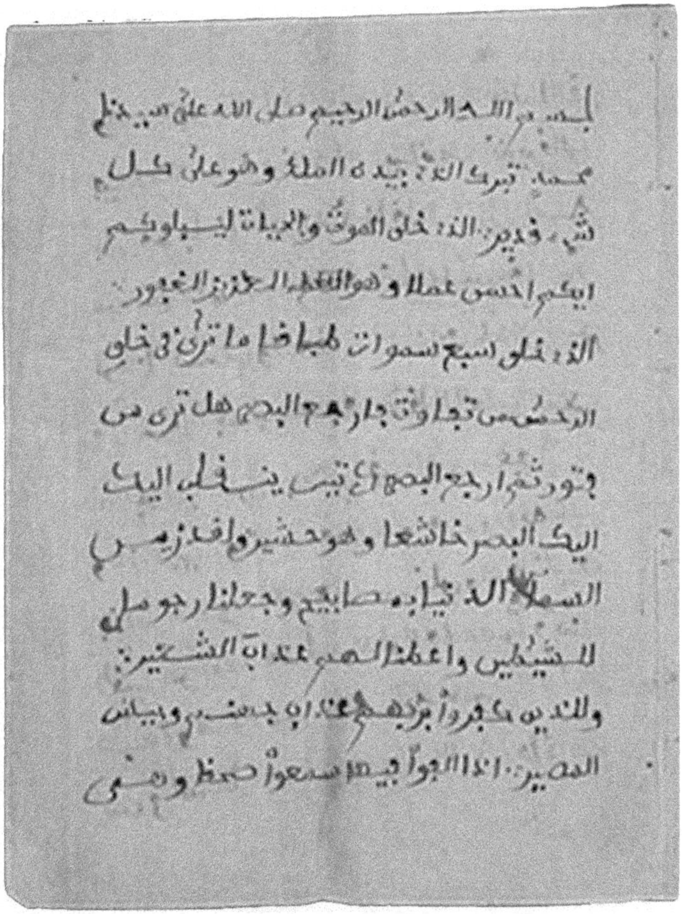

*Image: 9 Qur'anic Passages Written in Captivity.
Faith reduced to memory finds form again. These
lines are not argument. They are structure restored
where structure was denied.*

Chapter: 3 The Ocean

The ocean does not merely carry bodies; it rearranges time, memory, and survival.

Quote:

"We were placed upon a great ship and carried across the vast water."

The Hold.
The ocean received him through the ship, not as arrival but as descent, guided downward into a space designed to be filled rather than entered, where bodies were lowered in sequence and arranged without pause or acknowledgment. He was bound and pressed into the hold through a narrow opening, and the change in air was immediate, thick with breath already spent, warm, damp, and heavy with the residue of those placed below before him.

Light diminished rapidly as he moved downward, rationed by the structure of the vessel itself, while above decks remained active with movement and command.

The ship accepted bodies as cargo, measuring space by capacity rather than need, and the hold was constructed accordingly, with low beams and shelves that prevented standing and restricted sitting, forcing spines into permanent curve and limbs into fixed angles.

Posture, once taught and corrected, became impossible. Men were laid side by side, sometimes stacked on tiers, positioned to maximize number rather than survival, with shackles securing ankles or wrists to limit movement and prevent resistance.

Heat accumulated quickly and had nowhere to escape. Sweat soaked skin and wood alike, and evaporation was impossible in air already saturated. Waste collected beneath bodies or between them, and the smell became constant, no longer distinguishable as separate from breathing itself. Time lost all familiar reference.

There was no sunrise to mark beginning, no sunset to indicate closure. The hold existed in continuous darkness broken only when hatches opened briefly for inspection, feeding, or removal.

Image: 10   The Africans of the Slave Bark 'Wildfire Death entered the hold without ceremony. A body ceased responding. Breath failed. Those nearby knew before anyone above did. Removal followed when convenient, efficient and brief. Space closed immediately. The

Hunger arrived without schedule. Food was lowered in containers, distributed without concern for fairness or strength, and taken quickly by those able to reach it.

Water was rationed deliberately, enough to keep bodies alive but insufficient to restore strength, forcing the body to adjust by reducing expectation rather than resisting deprivation. Thirst became a condition rather than an episode, endured alongside pressure and heat. The discipline that had once governed his days no longer had external form, but it did not disappear.

Prayer continued inwardly, stripped of posture, washing, and direction, reduced to memory and repetition without sound. Words once spoken aloud now moved silently through recall, and structure survived where physical form could not. Sound within the hold changed over time. At first there were cries and protests, sharp and uncontrolled, rising instinctively when bodies encountered restraint and confinement. As days passed, cries diminished into groans, lower and measured, conserving energy.

Eventually, silence settled, not because suffering ended, but because expression produced no change. Silence became shared, dense and heavy, pressed between bodies as tightly as the bodies themselves. Movement was minimal and regulated by constraint rather than choice.

Those placed near the edges or ventilation slats fared marginally better, while those deeper within the hold endured greater heat and reduced air, and the difference was understood without being spoken. Disease spread quickly in such conditions, carried by proximity, filth, and weakened bodies. Diarrhea, fever, and respiratory distress appeared without distinction, and those affected were unable to isolate themselves or receive care.

Death entered without ceremony. A body ceased responding. Breath slowed, then stopped. Those nearest recognized it first, not by sight but by the change in weight and stillness beside them. Removal occurred when noticed by those above or when the smell forced acknowledgment.

27

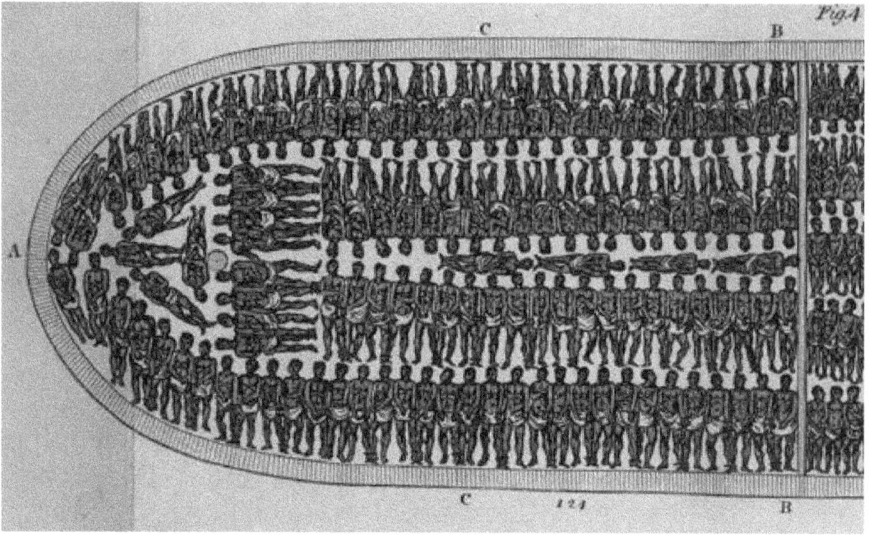

Image: 11 A late 18th-century abolitionist engraving showing the plan of a slave ship,

A hatch opened, chains loosened, and the body was taken out with efficiency. Space closed immediately.

There was no allowance for absence, no adjustment to reduce crowding. The arrangement tightened as if nothing had changed. The ship continued forward, indifferent to individual failure, governed by schedules of wind and profit rather than human endurance.

Within the hold, survival became collective in proximity but solitary in experience, each man confined not only by iron and wood but by the limits imposed on breath, movement, and attention.
The ocean outside remained unseen by most below, known only through the ship's motion and the damp air drawn inward, and the crossing progressed not as a single event but as an accumulation of days without markers.

By the time the body adapted to the conditions of the hold, it did so by lowering expectation to the narrow boundaries allowed, conserving thought, guarding memory, and enduring without anticipation of relief.
The ship moved forward without regard for those confined within it, driven by a sea that neither recognized nor responded to human presence, its motion governing heat, sickness, and survival alike.

When the water lay calm, the air in the hold stagnated, trapping warmth, breath, and disease until bodies weakened further under conditions that offered no release.
When storms rose, the vessel turned violent, pitching without warning, throwing bound bodies against one another and against the wooden frame, producing bruises and injury without distinction.

Sleep came only in fragments, interrupted by rolling motion, nausea, and the involuntary shifts of men pressed too closely together to separate their suffering.
He did not measure the crossing by days or scenes, but by endurance alone, preserving one fact that could withstand the overload of sensation: a month and a half at sea.

That number remained because numbers endured where detail dissolved. When the ship finally slowed and its motion changed, when unfamiliar smells entered the air and sound from above altered in tone, nothing within him recognized the moment as arrival.

By then, the hold had already completed its instruction. It had stripped away expectation, trained the body to persist without relief, and fixed the conditions of captivity so firmly that crossing from water to land did not register as transition, only continuation.

Bodies, Time, Silence

Cries rose at first without restraint, sharp and uncontrolled, the body announcing what the mind had not yet accepted, but they shortened quickly, pulled back before fully forming as men learned that sound carried consequence. Speech became risk. Any noise invited attention, and attention invited correction. Silence proved safer.

It conserved breath and strength and allowed a man to remain present without being marked. Within that silence, memory continued its work. Words once spoken aloud moved through the mind without sound, rehearsed carefully to prevent disappearance.

Names were repeated inwardly, not as comfort but as maintenance. Prayers adjusted to confinement, stripped of posture, washing, and movement, reduced to intention alone. Discipline learned in open spaces adapted to darkness and compression; the form was gone, but the structure held.

Death did not interrupt time in the hold. It was absorbed into it. A body ceased responding, and those pressed against it felt the change through weight and stillness before sight confirmed it. The space was reclaimed quickly. The living shifted without discussion.

There was no room for grief to unfold, because grief required space and time, and neither was permitted. Above them, the sea continued without reference to those it carried. When it lay calm, heat thickened and breathing became labor.

When it turned violent, the ship pitched suddenly, throwing bodies together and against wood, bruising heads and limbs that could not be protected. The sea did not distinguish between suffering and survival.

Image: 12 Storm at sea: shipwreck and chaos

It moved according to its own laws, and those laws were final. In that darkness, a man learned what remained when nearly everything else was removed.

The body learned endurance without expectation of relief. Time became something to be endured rather than measured. Silence became possession, one of the few things that could not be taken or exchanged.

By the time the ship's motion changed and unfamiliar scents filtered down through the hatch, those below were no longer waiting for the crossing to end. They had already learned how to exist within it.

Arrival Without Arrival

The ship slowed, and the change registered in the body before it could be named, the constant motion easing into irregular movement as the deck responded differently beneath weight trained to sway without instruction.

Voices above sharpened and multiplied, no longer measured by control but by anticipation, and new smells pushed into the hold—earth, smoke, refuse of a different sort—signals that the crossing had ended without clarifying what followed.

Light entered abruptly when the hatch opened, harsh and unmediated, striking eyes accustomed to darkness, and men were driven upward in sequence, limbs stiff from confinement, balance unreliable, hands guided to rails that existed for control rather than support.

 The sky appeared without transition, wide and indifferent, offering no recognition. The ocean lay behind them, yet its rhythm remained embedded in muscle and bone, the body continuing to adjust to motion that had ceased.

They were brought onto land, but nothing inside them registered arrival. Men stood exposed and unsteady, marked by salt, heat, and weeks without space, their bodies altered by confinement and deprivation. Visibility did not confer acknowledgment. It invited assessment.

Hands examined arms and backs. Eyes measured strength and condition. Teeth were checked. Age was guessed.

Value was assigned. The habits and discipline that had shaped him for decades found no application here. Knowledge carried no weight.

Memory had no currency. Silence, which had preserved him below, now read as absence rather than control. Language failed again.

The words spoken around him were not meant to invite reply or establish understanding. They moved quickly, sharply, serving transactions rather than communication. Commands were issued without explanation. Names were unnecessary.

He understood enough to recognize that comprehension itself no longer mattered. The body was the sole subject of interest. Everything else could be disregarded. He recorded the event without elaboration: after the crossing, they came to a place called Charleston. He did not describe relief or safety. He did not treat land as refuge.

Ground functioned as another mechanism, a surface on which ownership could be transferred efficiently. The sea had delivered them to a system already prepared to receive them. Sale followed without ceremony. The crossing had thinned bodies and reduced resistance.

The market completed the process. Men were separated, repositioned, passed from one set of hands to another, the brief collective endurance of the hold dissolving immediately. Survival had been shared below out of necessity. On land it became solitary by design.

The ship receded from view, but the sensation of water did not leave the body.

Image: 13 Arrival and Sale A new land enters the record without welcome. Ownership replaces movement. Names appear not as belonging, but as claim.

The residual sway persisted, balance lagging behind stillness. Arrival had occurred geographically, but nothing settled internally.

He stood on land that did not recognize him and did not intend to learn who he was. This was not a beginning. It was continuation under a different arrangement.

The ocean released him only enough to pass him forward, and the world beyond the dock claimed what the water had prepared, proceeding without curiosity, without pause, and without acknowledgment that anything had crossed except cargo.

Chapter: 4 Unread Country

Introduction: Arrival does not always mean belonging; sometimes it only marks possession.

Quote:

"I was sold, and another man's name replaced my own."

Sale

Sale did not announce itself with noise because noise was no longer required; the crossing had already reduced men to condition, and here the process continued with practiced calm refined through repetition. Bodies were positioned where light could reach them, turned and held so muscle, height, and visible strength could be evaluated quickly, while weakness was noted without comment. Men stood not to be addressed but to be assessed.

The ground beneath their feet was solid again, yet it offered no grounding, because stability belonged only to those who possessed it. Hands reached without request or acknowledgment. Arms were lifted, jaws opened, teeth inspected with an efficiency that bordered on contempt. Limbs were pressed and released. Eyes traveled rapidly, lingering only on what translated directly into labor.

Age was guessed without care for accuracy. Strength was assumed where it could be extracted. Silence, once protective, was read as emptiness rather than restraint. No one asked who a man had been before the water carried him. No one asked what discipline had shaped his days or what knowledge he carried intact.

That information had no place in the transaction. Words passed around him like weather, heard but not engaged, and understanding them would not have altered the result. The language of sale was not designed to communicate but to conclude. Numbers replaced names.

Image: 14 Inspection and sale, nineteenth century A period engraving recording examination prior to sale. Such images document procedure and possession, not consent or identity.

Gestures replaced consent. Ownership shifted from one hand to another with the same ease as breath moves through a crowded space, unnoticed and unremarked.

He was purchased and later described with a precision that did not soften with time: small in stature, physically weak, and cruel, a man without fear of the Lord.

This judgment did not arise from emotion but from immediate recognition, because a man who answers to nothing beyond himself recognizes no limit, and where cruelty may pause under restraint, godlessness does not. The transaction ended without ceremony.

Attention moved on. Another body was brought forward. The rhythm continued without interruption. There was no marker for the moment his life was reassigned, no threshold crossed, no pause allowed for orientation or resistance.

He was led away as property transferred between accounts rather than a man entering a new place. The land did not acknowledge him. The people did not see him.

The country did not read him. It registered possession, use, and control, and nothing beyond that. Sale did not introduce captivity. It confirmed what had already been enforced through movement, deprivation, and erasure.

From that point forward, his restraint would be mistaken for compliance, his silence for absence, and his survival for consent.

The market did not need to understand him to take him. It required only the decision of where to send him next.

Image: 15   A 19th-century engraving titled "Slaves Waiting for Sale, Virginia."

The Small Wicked Man

The man who purchased him in Charleston was not remembered as a figure of scale or reputation but as a man whose smallness shaped his rule, because in a system built on ownership, physical weakness often translated into heightened cruelty used deliberately to enforce obedience.

Omar names him Johnson and records his judgment without embellishment: a man without fear of the Lord, and therefore without internal restraint, a condition Omar recognized immediately as dangerous, because where no higher accountability is acknowledged, there is no limit on what may be done to another human being.

Charleston itself marked no beginning; it functioned as a sorting mechanism, a port organized for transfer rather than transition, its air thick with tar, salt, damp timber, and the concentrated pressure of commerce where bodies were assessed with the same scrutiny as goods.

Omar was moved quickly from the ship into Johnson's possession, not as a man formed by years of disciplined study and ordered life, but as a unit of labor expected to produce immediate return.

The language spoken around him was clipped and transactional, delivered without interest in response, and though he did not understand the words, he understood their function, because ownership operates without need for translation. Johnson's world was intentionally narrow: confined spaces, limited movement, rules enforced through repetition and threat, an environment designed to prevent disappearance, delay, or negotiation.

Such men required control to be visible and constant, because authority unsupported by moral restraint depended entirely on fear.

Labor was demanded immediately, without allowance for recovery from the crossing or adjustment to the land, as though a body stripped by weeks in the hold could be reshaped instantly into a tool. Omar states the central problem plainly and without excuse: he was a small man and unable to perform heavy labor. This was not a claim for mercy but a factual limitation, and in a system that treated capacity as value, such limitations invited punishment rather than accommodation.

During that first month, he learned the local rhythm of captivity, which followed neither sun nor season but demand. Sleep occurred only when permitted. Waking followed command rather than necessity. Food was issued as control rather than sustenance, and humiliation was administered alongside labor as reinforcement.

The body was required to continue even when weakened. The mind was expected to submit even when it recognized the difference between authority grounded in order and force applied without restraint. There existed no legal language available to him, no council to appeal to, no elder to intervene, no teacher to correct excess.

Violence functioned as the only corrective mechanism, and it corrected only one outcome: continued compliance. Omar does not catalogue the abuses of that household in detail. Instead, he defines its moral boundary. He calls Johnson wicked. He identifies him as an infidel.

He states plainly that the man did not fear the Lord at all. In Omar's framework, this was not an insult but a diagnostic conclusion, a way of stating that nothing imposed a ceiling on behavior within that house, because when reverence is absent, appetite becomes law and cruelty remains unchecked by consequence.

الحمد لله الذي خلق الخلق للعبادة ثم جرى حتى جرى على أوجاعهم وأقوالهم وأحوالهم وأديانهم
بلغ السلام في مبدئ وغوفى وما معهم في جماعة الحق في كل ملك ترى بستى
زولي وأولاد الهي بلا به إلا ذاط بلا ذاط بلا أقول من بعد أقتح انقول
جمعنا قول صورة الحق و ولا نشرفه نص بأي بحال فقد خمس الوجل بأن ينزلها
وبلا ماذا عبرا با أزا بيا أو خمرت أوابو سعد جاز ألبرخة الله لا تخبر بيد

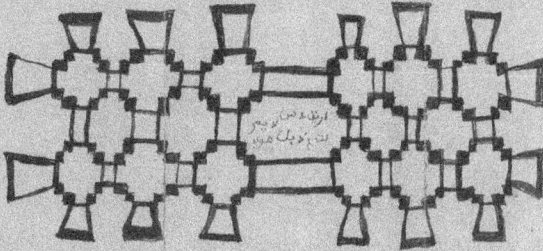

نوويه جوزة انيس محمد ازنا تيس الحمد الله و ولا الله ذلك الذي اذا افسد
للمي أن هي الاسماء همينهمر والنذر وإبك حكم إبك ذار الله بهما
الخبر عند الله لا تخبر بت بكا اب لهبروت ما أغنى عنه ما له وما

بهذا الذكر بالله بأن من شاب ما انتفاع لا بل المعتبر يا أخي من ملك م
اوانت مجنون اوانت اهمى لك وشع زوولد الشو كى كى د

أقول من بعد

Image: 16 Manuscript Page with Autobiographical Lines The life appears briefly, without ornament. Education, capture, and removal are named without explanation. Silence surrounds the facts, not because they were small, but because endurance does not need emphasis

43

Life under such a man did not offer gradual adjustment or negotiated endurance; it offered escalation. Faced with this, Omar did not dramatize his response. He did not describe

confrontation or appeal. He recorded only the necessary action that remained within his power. He fled from the hand of Johnson. The phrasing is deliberate. He was not escaping a building or a city but a grip, an ownership that renewed itself daily through threat.

Flight was not framed as courage or victory but as necessity, a decision made when the known future had already declared itself intolerable.

He left without provision or plan sufficient to ensure safety, because remaining guaranteed harm. This act introduced the next consequence in his life: capture within a system that allowed no margin for unsanctioned movement.

He was seized again shortly after fleeing and confined in the jail at Fayetteville, North Carolina, where the local authorities held him as a runaway slave, an offense defined entirely by possession rather than conduct.

The jail was small, built for containment rather than reflection, its walls thick, its interior dark, and its purpose singular. Here, the discipline that had survived the crossing resurfaced in altered form. Deprived of speech and agency,

Omar turned inward and wrote Arabic words from memory on the walls, verses and prayers recalled without text, an act that drew attention precisely because literacy in that form was unexpected.

This writing did not secure his freedom, but it altered the course of his captivity by making him legible to observers who could not read his words but recognized their significance.

From this point forward, his life would proceed through transfers rather than choices, shaped by the interpretations others imposed on what they could not fully understand.

The flight from Johnson did not end captivity, but it marked the first recorded instance in which Omar acted directly against ownership rather than within it, establishing a pattern that would continue in quieter forms: resistance through preservation, through writing, through memory carried intact even when the body was constrained.

Fear as Law

Fear did not enter his life as spectacle or sudden terror but as a governing system that embedded itself into routine and learned the shape of the hours, pressing when it served its purpose and withdrawing when withdrawal preserved its power, until obedience felt inevitable rather than coerced. In that house, fear did not announce itself loudly; it observed, waited, and corrected without explanation, becoming the rule that replaced every other structure of order.

The man who owned him did not govern through consistency but through deliberate uncertainty, altering expectations without warning and shifting boundaries without cause, a method designed to prevent prediction and therefore resistance. What was permitted one day invited punishment the next, not through confusion but intention, because a body that cannot anticipate consequence learns to reduce itself, and a mind that cannot locate mercy learns to retreat inward.

Labor was demanded without regard for physical capacity, as though a body weakened by the Atlantic crossing could immediately be converted into an instrument of production, and when that body failed to meet expectation, failure was defined not as limitation but as defiance. Correction followed not to instruct or improve but to reinforce dominance, administered with enough frequency to remain credible but enough irregularity to remain feared. Fear did not need to be constant to be effective; it needed only to be possible at all times, and possibility carried the discipline forward without effort. Omar identified his owner's danger not through emotional language but through moral diagnosis, recording that the man did not fear the Lord at all, a conclusion rooted in observation rather than sentiment, because a man who recognizes no authority beyond himself acknowledges no boundary, and where no boundary exists, appetite becomes law.

This absence of reverence was not abstract but operational, visible in the way punishment was applied when it served convenience and withheld when restraint preserved

strength for later use, in the way hunger was deployed as pressure and sleep rationed without explanation, and in the way bodies were driven past usefulness and then blamed for their collapse. Mercy appeared only by accident, never as principle, and those subjected to this rule learned quickly that kindness could not be trusted because it did not bind future behavior. The house did not erupt in constant rage; it functioned through calculation, because calculated fear lasts longer than uncontrolled violence and produces compliance without exhausting the hand that applies it. In such a place, devotion was mocked, restraint was misread as weakness, and silence was taken as permission rather than discipline.

Nothing higher than immediate authority was acknowledged, and nothing final was feared, creating an environment where action proceeded as though no accounting would ever be required. There was no appeal available within this system, no law that stood between the hand and the body, no witness whose presence altered outcome, because the house answered only to itself. Omar recognized this immediately, and his recognition followed a precise logic: he did not begin by describing individual acts of cruelty but by identifying the absence of moral restraint that made those acts unlimited.

A man without fear of the Lord fears nothing else, and a man who fears nothing else recognizes no limit. Under such conditions, fear becomes not a response but the governing principle itself. Sleep offered no refuge, arriving lightly and fragmenting easily, because waking could bring arbitrary punishment or renewed demand, training the body to rest without surrender and the mind to remain alert even in stillness.

Image: 17 Qur'anic Invocation in Omar's Script Sacred words carried long before ink was allowed to receive them. What appears here was memorized when books were still possible, preserved when they were not.

Silence was maintained not out of humility but survival, because speech invited attention, attention invited correction, and correction invited pain without instruction. Time itself was reordered around proximity to danger rather than obligation or rhythm, measured not by sun or task but by the likelihood of interference, and every movement was calculated while every stillness was assessed.

The discipline that had once structured his life was not extinguished but compressed into vigilance, narrowed to fit an environment where visible devotion could be interpreted as defiance. Faith did not disappear, but it was forced inward, practiced without outward sign, preserved as intention rather than form in order to survive a context that recognized only obedience. This existence did not constitute a life but a condition, one defined by management rather than purpose, and Omar understood with the clarity of a man trained to recognize systems that remaining within it would not result in endurance but in erasure. Fear as law does not aim to sustain a body; it aims to extract usefulness until compliance breaks and replacement becomes necessary.

When he chose to flee, the act did not arise from impulse or rebellion but from recognition, an assessment grounded in the understanding that the known future under such authority offered only escalation. He did not run from a location or a momentary threat but from a hand that claimed unlimited authority, because fear left unchallenged would have authored the remainder of his life without reference to his existence beyond utility.

Flight represented the last action still under his control, not as assertion of dominance but as refusal to surrender the interior self to a system that denied its reality. In that decision, he obeyed a law older and more binding than fear itself, the law that a man must not consent inwardly to a structure that recognizes no soul, even when the body remains constrained by force.

Chapter: 5 Flight

Flight is not always toward freedom, but away from certainty of destruction.

Quote:

"I ran because remaining had already decided my end."

Escape Without Direction

He did not plan escape with foresight or destination because there was no future available within the place he occupied, only a narrowing present that made remaining impossible, and the decision formed not as courage or strategy but as recognition that staying would complete the work fear had begun. He fled not from a building or a road but from a hand that exercised unlimited authority, and the moment arrived without signal, created by a brief absence of attention that would not repeat itself. He moved when movement became possible rather than safe, the body acting before the mind could calculate consequence, and fear did not disappear in flight but changed function, pushing motion instead of enforcing stillness.

He ran without direction, not toward refuge or promise, but away from certainty, placing distance between himself and what had already declared its intention. The land offered no guidance beyond concealment and separation, with paths dissolving into fields, fields breaking into woods, and order appearing briefly before vanishing again. He did not know where he was going and did not attempt to decide it, knowing only where he could not remain, and that knowledge was sufficient to sustain movement through exhaustion and uncertainty.

Days passed without alignment to memory, nights provided cover without rest, and sleep came lightly, shaped by alertness rather than recovery. Discipline remained present even in flight, expressed not as ritual but as restraint, with breath controlled, movement measured, and panic refused because panic wasted strength.

He stopped only when stopping could no longer be postponed and moved again when rest had been exhausted, because delay invited capture and hesitation closed openings that did not reopen. Hunger arrived without spectacle and remained without apology, hollowing the body gradually until walking required intention rather than instinct. The stomach learned to remain empty without protest, and weakness spread slowly, forcing muscles to ration effort as breath had once been rationed in confinement. Food appeared infrequently and was taken without ceremony, whatever could be consumed quickly and unseen, because nourishment had become permission to continue rather than restoration. Water was seized when available, not measured or spared, because the body no longer assumed abundance or continuity.

Prayer returned not as form but as alignment, silent and inward, stripped of posture and direction and reduced to intention carried through motion, while memory worked steadily under strain, preserving language and names without allowing them to surface into sound. Distance accumulated without markers, each step increasing separation from the certainty of recapture without offering clarity in return.

Roads hinted at structure and then dissolved, houses appeared at intervals offering neither invitation nor safety, and he avoided light and followed shadow not because darkness promised refuge but because visibility invited attention.

Image: 18 Chains of sorrow and prayer

Distance became a fragile shelter, thin and temporary but necessary, stretched between the body and the authority that sought to reclaim it.

Flight did not restore freedom or offer resolution but interrupted erasure, holding space open long enough for survival to continue.
He walked because stopping meant capture and continued because return guaranteed submission, accepting that direction would come later, if it came at all, and that for now movement itself was sufficient because it preserved the one remaining authority still available to him, the refusal to remain where fear functioned as law and the soul was treated as excess.

Sleep came in pieces, short and shallow rests taken where the land allowed concealment, and the body learned to rise quickly, to wake without confusion, and to listen before moving. Fear did not leave him but refined itself into awareness sharpened into habit, the constant measuring of sound, movement, and proximity, carried as a tool rather than a paralysis.

Silence was maintained deliberately, not as submission but as protection, because speech invited attention and attention invited pursuit. Prayer persisted as insistence rather than appeal, practiced without water or space, without standing or bowing, and without reliable direction, yet the inner order did not vanish.

Words shaped themselves inwardly and were carried without sound, held carefully so they would not fracture under exhaustion.
Alignment was maintained through intention and memory rather than posture, through refusal to allow chaos to claim the inner hours completely.

Prayer did not ask for rescue or deliverance; it asked for endurance sufficient to continue. Each day without capture felt provisional, each night without pursuit felt borrowed, and he did not imagine safety waiting ahead, only the next step, the next concealment, the next interval in which he could remain unseen.

The discipline learned long before sustained him now not by promising relief but by teaching him how to persist without it. Hunger thinned him, distance isolated him, and prayer held what remained together.

When his strength began to falter in ways discipline could no longer correct and the body signaled that flight could not continue indefinitely, he did not interpret the limit as failure but recognized it as boundary, understanding that even endurance has edges, and that somewhere ahead, without his knowing it yet, this boundary would force the next turning and carry him into another phase of captivity shaped by consequence rather than choice.

The Church Door

He reached the door not as destination but as limit, his strength reduced to warning, legs unsteady, breath shortening without effort, the body signaling that flight could not continue without collapse, and he entered that place not by choice but because there was nowhere else to go. The building stood heavier than the houses he had avoided, raised with intention rather than convenience, constructed to endure and to gather, and though he did not know its name in their language, he recognized its function immediately as a space set apart from labor and trade. He later recalled that he went into a church to pray, recording the act plainly without embellishment, because prayer for him did not depend on form or permission but on alignment when all other structures had failed.

Time had been damaged by capture and flight, but it had not vanished, and whatever internal markers remained guided him toward stillness rather than concealment. He entered quietly and without announcement, taking a position where he could stand without drawing attention, aligning himself inwardly as best he could, offering prayer without posture or sound, intent held where words were unnecessary. He did not know he was observed.

A child noticed him first, recognizing difference without understanding it, and left quickly, as children do when uncertainty demands action. Omar remained unaware, holding himself together long enough to finish what he had begun, his attention narrowed to breath and memory rather than surroundings. Dogs arrived before men, the sound cutting through the interior and transforming the space from quiet to signal, and with that sound the door ceased to function as refuge and became instead a point of identification.

Men followed, mounted and certain, using the dogs to close distance quickly, and Omar did not run, not from resignation but because the body had already stated its limit and resistance would have altered nothing.

56

He was taken without ceremony, seized and removed from the place he had entered seeking alignment rather than protection, carried back under authority rather than distance. He later recorded that he was taken about twelve miles and placed in the jail at Fayetteville, North Carolina, a town already organized to receive such returns, its jail built for containment rather than deliberation.

The church receded behind him, not as failure but as interruption, the moment when flight ended not only in capture but in visibility. He would state the sequence simply: he entered a church to pray, a boy saw him, men came with dogs and took him away.

He offered no complaint and no appeal to irony. The door had not saved him, but it had marked a transition. From that moment, he would no longer move unseen. He had crossed into a system that would insist on naming him, counting him, confining him again under rules broader than the fear of one man.

The law that closed around him now was not the private violence of a household but the public machinery of custody, and it carried him into a cell where the discipline that had survived capture, the road, the hold, and flight would reappear in altered form.

The church door closed behind him, and the next door that received him was iron, set within thick walls, its purpose singular. What followed would not depend on escape or concealment but on what could be preserved when movement ended and attention returned, when silence became visible again and endurance had to find a new shape.

Image: 19 Qur'anic Invocation in Omar's Script Sacred words carried long before ink was allowed to receive them. What appears here was memorized when books were still possible, preserved when they were not.

Chapter: 6 The Jail

Flight is not always toward freedom, but away from certainty of destruction.

Quote:

"I ran because remaining had already decided my end."

Stone, Iron, Noise

The building closed around him with a finality the road had never imposed, stone replacing distance and ending movement completely, its thickness designed to contain rather than guide, to absorb sound and prevent the outside world from entering with clarity. The door shut once and did not invite reconsideration, and the walls did what they were built to do, pressing inward until the body understood that motion now belonged to others. Iron followed stone. Bars defined the room without ambiguity, catching light without warmth and establishing limits as fact rather than warning.

The floor held cold regardless of the air, offering no accommodation, no surface that allowed the body to settle, so that standing exhausted the legs, sitting numbed them, and lying down failed to restore anything beyond momentary stillness. Architecture dictated posture and denied comfort by design, and the body learned quickly that endurance here meant accepting imbalance rather than seeking relief.

Noise replaced the silence that had once protected him, not the sudden noise of pursuit or the sharp commands of capture, but the continuous noise of confinement, a layered presence that never fully receded. Voices passed through walls without clarity, chains answered one another in adjacent spaces, doors opened and closed according to rhythms he could not anticipate, and men shouted, laughed, argued, and cursed beyond reach, their sounds colliding and dissolving before meaning could form.

Night altered the pitch but not the presence of this noise, and quiet never fully arrived. He did not understand the words spoken around him, but he understood the indifference that carried them. This was a place where explanation was unnecessary because purpose did not require participation.

A man was held because holding him served an external function, and that function did not depend on his comprehension. Presence was sufficient. He later recorded the duration with care: sixteen days and nights in the jail at Fayetteville.

The number mattered because time here did not dissolve as it had on the road or at sea. It hardened. Each day pressed down distinctly, identical yet weighted with awareness, marked by the regular return of hunger and the predictable absence of choice.

Food arrived according to schedule rather than need, water according to policy rather than condition, and the repetition itself enforced submission more efficiently than threat. The discipline he carried did not collapse under this pressure.

It adapted. There was no space to wash properly, no reliable direction that could be chosen without exposure, and no opportunity to perform prayer as form, yet lignment persisted. Words were held silently and repeated inwardly, intention replacing posture, memory supplying what circumstance denied.

The walls could contain the body, but they could not reorganize the inner hours, and within those hours order continued to function, stripped of outward sign but intact in sequence and restraint. Stone, iron, and noise became the grammar of the place, speaking constantly of limit and custody, reminding him that his presence here was not temporary by design but provisional by decision not yet revealed. Waiting became labor.

Not passive waiting, but the sustained effort of remaining intact while nothing changed, of holding attention without outlet and endurance without movement. Even before the door opened again, the jail accomplished a transition that mattered

Image: 20 The prisoner and his watchers . Thirst arrived on schedule. Sleep came reluctantly, broken by sound and light and the constant knowledge that rest here was provisional.

It replaced pursuit with possession and flight with suspension. The world narrowed deliberately, no longer uneven and uncertain as it had been during escape, but fixed and administered, and whatever followed would emerge from behind walls rather than along a road.

The stone did not ask his name, and the iron did not require it, because identification here was administrative rather than personal.

Silence, which had once functioned as concealment, now had to be recalibrated, because in a place where noise was constant, silence became visible, a deviation noticed by those trained to watch.

He learned to exist within sound without reacting to it, to let it pass without drawing him outward, maintaining inward order while outward control was absolute. When the door finally opened, it did so without gentleness, but by then the jail had already completed its work, establishing the terms under which he would be seen and managed next. He would move again, but not as a fugitive.

He would be transferred, interpreted, and reassigned within a structure that recognized custody as normal and containment as routine. The period of sixteen days did not free him, but it clarified the nature of what followed, because it demonstrated that survival now depended less on movement and more on preservation under observation. The road had demanded endurance through motion.

The jail demanded endurance through stillness. In that shift, the discipline that had carried him across land and water found a new application, not as resistance or appeal, but as the steady maintenance of self where architecture, authority, and noise were designed to dissolve it.

Writing on the Walls

The walls did not respond, and that made them safe, because stone does not interrupt, does not correct, and does not punish a man for choosing the wrong word, receiving whatever is pressed into it without judgment, and in a place governed by iron, keys, and sound where voices carried authority and silence could draw attention, the walls became the only surface that did not answer back.

He began to write because not writing would have meant surrendering something that could not be recovered once lost, and there was no ink prepared for him, no desk offered, no permission granted, the act itself unsanctioned and therefore precise in its meaning. His hand moved cautiously at first, recalling forms held for decades, letters remembered before polish, sense returning before grammar, the language rising unevenly through fatigue and hunger, and he knew even as he wrote that the hand was weaker, the eyes strained, the language imperfect, a fact he would later acknowledge without drama, but none of that diminished the necessity of the act.

He wrote words of the Divine not to instruct a reader or argue belief, but to restore orientation, to anchor himself against a system that reduced time to noise and authority to force, to remind himself that power did not originate with men who held keys and that creation remained governed by laws older than stone walls and iron doors. The writing was not decoration and not performance; it was structure, each line restoring sequence where the jail imposed sameness, each word pressed into the wall resisting the flattening of hours into indistinguishable confinement, the act itself reintroducing order where none was provided.

The body remained confined, but the mind stepped back into a pattern it recognized, and that recognition mattered because survival here depended less on movement than on preservation under observation.

He wrote knowing the markings might be erased, that guards might remove them or whitewash the surface, but erasure had already occurred on larger scales, and permanence was not the point; continuity was. A man who stops rehearsing what shapes him does not remain intact, and the walls allowed rehearsal without interruption. What he wrote drew from memory rather than text, passages long memorized during years of study, words carried across land and sea and confinement without paper, including invocations and chapters known by heart, written now not for accuracy of presentation but for maintenance of order.

Later observers would note this with surprise, a jailed African man writing sacred words in Arabic on an American jail wall, treating it as novelty or curiosity, but none of that existed in the moment; here there was only necessity. The writing was not for those who might later read it. It was for survival in a space designed to dissolve interior life through noise, repetition, and enforced passivity.

Outside the cell, sound continued without pattern he could predict, doors opening and closing, chains moving, voices rising and falling, but none of it entered the lines forming beneath his hand. Inside the writing, order held while the world beyond remained governed by impatience and force. He did not write his own story yet, did not record events or grievance, because that would come later, when asked, when pressed, when explanation would be required. Here he wrote what had shaped him long before anyone claimed him, because stone would not interrupt and because walls, unlike men, could be trusted to keep what was given to them without argument.

In this quiet and unauthorized act, the jail failed in one crucial way: it contained his body but did not contain his memory, and by allowing that memory to be rehearsed and fixed against the wall, he preserved the internal order that captivity depended on erasing.

Being Seen

The door opened without warning and light entered before explanation, spreading across stone and iron and settling on him as if he had been positioned deliberately to be found, and with the light came voices, not sharp with command but clustered with curiosity, overlapping in a way that signaled attention rather than threat. The quiet he had learned to inhabit fractured under that attention, because for the first time since capture he was not simply contained; he was observed. Men gathered at the threshold and did not rush him or raise their hands but stood looking, their stillness weighted with assessment, and their eyes moved past his body almost immediately to the walls behind him, where the writing drew them before any question could form.

They pointed, spoke to one another, leaned closer, then withdrew, circling marks they could not read and lines they could not place, a language that did not belong to the space they believed they controlled. He did not explain himself, because explanation required authority he did not possess and because silence had preserved him until now. He remained where he stood, small and enclosed, his body offering nothing remarkable, while the walls carried evidence that something within him had not been reduced in the manner expected.

Names were spoken, perhaps his, perhaps others, but he did not recognize them and did not respond, and confusion moved through the group not as anger but as disturbance, because a man who could not be classified unsettled the order they trusted. Property was meant to be legible, predictable, and immediately assignable, and this was not. One man stepped forward and gestured toward the walls, tracing shapes without comprehension, while another asked something in a questioning tone rather than a demand, and he did not answer, not out of refusal but

because the words did not carry meaning for him. Language failed again, but this time its failure shifted the center of gravity away from him and toward those watching, forcing them to speak among themselves, to interpret and speculate. Being seen did not bring relief. It brought exposure. He had written to survive the jail, to preserve internal order in a place designed to dissolve it, and now that writing had altered the terms of his captivity. He was no longer merely a body held for return or transfer; he had become an anomaly, a curiosity that disrupted expectation, something that required explanation or removal. The walls that had kept his words safe from interruption had now delivered them into view, and the attention that followed carried consequence. Keys moved.

Decisions formed beyond his hearing and without his participation. He was led out, not with violence but with certainty, the way one moves something that can no longer be ignored without effort. The jail released him not because mercy had entered the calculation but because its purpose had been met. It had contained him, broken his flight, and revealed him. As he was taken away, the walls remained behind, still bearing the marks of his hand, and whether those markings would be erased or preserved no longer mattered, because they had already done what was required. They had made visible what captivity could not fully flatten. He had been seen, and that fact alone altered what followed, because once a man is seen in this way, silence can no longer function as concealment, and the next stage of his confinement would unfold under attention rather than neglect.

Image: 21 Qur'anic Invocation in Omar's Script Sacred words carried long before ink was allowed to receive them. What appears here was memorized when books were still possible, preserved when they were not.

Chapter: 7 Owned House

Confinement reveals what cannot be taken when the body is fully contained.

Quote:

"Stone and iron held me, but they did not hold what I remembered."

Clean Clothes, Unclean Truth

They changed his clothes before they changed his condition, replacing the rags of the jail with garments clean enough to satisfy inspection, stiff with newness and cut without regard for the body that would wear them, the smell of soap masking nothing beneath it except to the eye of those who believed appearance signaled resolution.

Hands adjusted the fabric not with care but with arrangement, preparing him for transfer from a cell that had revealed him as a problem into a household prepared to receive him as possession, because cleanliness here did not signify mercy but the reassertion of order. He was removed from the jail at Fayetteville after sixteen days and placed into the custody of James Owen, a planter and politician whose standing in North Carolina depended on reputation, propriety, and visible restraint rather than overt brutality. The change was immediate and instructive. The house Owen kept differed from the jail in structure and scale, with wider rooms, cleaner floors, and light that entered freely through open windows, yet the authority governing it was no less complete. Ownership did not require chains to announce itself. It settled into routine, expectation, and the unspoken certainty that another man's body now belonged inside these boundaries. He was placed rather than

welcomed, positioned within the household as a resource to be maintained rather than a presence to be acknowledged. Food arrived at regular intervals. Water was provided without struggle. Sleep extended beyond the fragments allowed in confinement. These were not gifts and were not framed as kindness. They were investments. A body that eats works longer. A body that rests obeys more efficiently. Comfort refined captivity without reducing it.

The truth of the arrangement revealed itself gradually, not through sudden violence but through calibrated behavior. Kindness appeared selectively, extended when it reinforced control and withdrawn when it risked encouraging autonomy. Instruction was delivered with patience that expected gratitude in return, tone replacing explanation, and compliance assumed rather than negotiated. Owen did not govern through volatility. He governed through predictability, a system that reduced resistance by minimizing friction. Where Johnson's house had relied on fear sharpened through uncertainty, this house relied on calm reinforced through dependence. Fear remained present, but it no longer shouted.

It watched. It reminded. In this environment, devotion became dangerous in a different way. What had been mocked or punished in the earlier household was now misread as harmless peculiarity. Prayer observed without disruption was interpreted as habit rather than allegiance. Silence was taken as simplicity. Restraint was mistaken for acceptance. The absence of visible resistance was read as internal agreement, a misunderstanding that both protected him and confined him more effectively than open hostility. He learned quickly that the danger here lay not in overt cruelty but in interpretation, because a man who believes himself benevolent rarely questions the limits of his authority.

Owen allowed him space to read and write, noting his literacy with interest rather than suspicion, an allowance that would later shape how Omar's faith and intellect were reframed within Christian terms by those around him. This accommodation did not weaken ownership. It stabilized it. By permitting selected expressions of difference, the household converted anomaly into managed curiosity, keeping him intact enough to be useful while rendering his inner life increasingly invisible to those who believed they understood him. Omar learned to move with precision, to

71

Image: 22 Daily chores at the plantation

accept what was given without revealing what was retained, to perform compliance without surrender. The discipline that had once ordered his life now served a different function. It allowed him to inhabit misinterpretation without dissolving under it.

He learned when to speak and when silence would be misread as virtue. He learned when prayer must retreat inward and when visible restraint would protect him from scrutiny.

Clean clothes rested against his skin, and regular meals strengthened his body, but the truth beneath remained distorted by ownership and misreading, by a system that believed improvement could substitute for freedom. This house did not intend to destroy him.

It intended to keep him, to preserve him as an object of order and evidence of paternal control, and that intention demanded vigilance no less exacting than cruelty. Calm authority required constant maintenance. Misunderstanding had to be sustained.

Gratitude had to be assumed. Within this structure, Omar remained captive not through pain but through containment, his survival dependent on navigating a world that believed itself just because it was not openly violent. The transition from jail to household did not restore agency. It replaced confinement with management, flight with supervision, erasure with misnaming.

He was no longer hunted, beaten, or starved, but he was no less owned, and the clarity of this arrangement shaped the remainder of his life, because from this point forward, captivity would be administered through care rather than fear, through interpretation rather than force, demanding from him a vigilance measured not in resistance but in preservation, as he learned to endure within a system that mistook its own restraint for righteousness and expected him to mistake survival for consent.

Kindness Without Freedom

The kindness he encountered did not present itself as manipulation but as certainty, a confidence that assumed its own goodness without needing to test it, comparing itself only to harsher examples and concluding that improvement was equivalent to justice. Voices softened, hands slowed, instructions were delivered with patience rather than threat, meals arrived at regular hours, and rest followed labor with predictable allowance, creating a household rhythm that congratulated itself quietly on its restraint.

Freedom was never discussed, not because it was denied explicitly, but because it was not imagined as a category that applied to him. Kindness operated comfortably within ownership, improving appearance without altering purpose, making captivity easier to endure and easier to forget without ever loosening its boundaries. He was observed with interest rather than suspicion, his restraint praised, his silence interpreted as humility, his discipline mistaken for consent, and the household translated what it saw through its own assumptions, reassuring itself that this was a reasonable arrangement, a calm man, a cooperative presence, proof that captivity could be administered without cruelty.

This misreading protected him in practical ways, creating space where none had existed before, space to breathe without fear of sudden violence, space to remember without immediate punishment, space to maintain inward order while outwardly conforming. He did not challenge the interpretation, understanding that correcting it would require authority he did not possess and would invite consequences he did not need.

Image: 23 Helping hands on the plantation

He was allowed near the children, not by declaration but by habit, left in rooms with them without warning or supervision, an unspoken judgment that he was contained enough to be considered safe, not free or equal, but manageable. He moved carefully among them, did not raise his voice, did not correct unless asked, and the household learned without discussion that nothing in him unsettled their sense of control.

Prayer remained quiet, not hidden but unannounced, practiced when attention softened and eyes turned elsewhere, the discipline that had once structured entire days now compressed into fragments carefully fitted between demands. Faith did not change its substance, only its visibility, adapting to a world that misinterpreted restraint as agreement. Kindness complicated vigilance.

Cruelty announces itself clearly and invites resistance; kindness blurs boundaries, asks for gratitude, and encourages the captive to believe endurance has been rewarded rather than managed. He did not confuse the two. His body rested more consistently, but his condition remained unchanged.

He understood what the household did not, that freedom is not defined by the absence of pain but by the absence of ownership, and that kindness offered without release refines control rather than dissolving it. The household believed it had improved him, when in fact it had only adjusted its methods. His understanding of faith had never been grounded in comfort. It had been formed through discipline long before capture, in a land where belief was learned through memory and repetition, structure and restraint, rising before the body wished to rise and submitting to order when resistance seemed easier. Prayer was learned as grammar, sequence as law, silence as reverence.

Scripture was not performed but carried, copied, corrected, returned to memory, erased, and written again until the hand obeyed the mind and the mind submitted to something older than both. This was the formation of scholars, not separate from labor but embedded within it. When he was taken, that formation did not leave him; it was pressed inward. Around him, many lost language, kinship, and permission to remember, beaten into forgetting, renamed until memory loosened, or surviving only through silence. He did not forget. He adjusted. What could no longer be spoken aloud was preserved exactly within.

What could not be practiced openly was practiced without witnesses. Form endured even when its name was denied. He lived within that adjustment deliberately, neither rejecting the conditions of survival nor surrendering to the interpretations imposed on him, holding himself together in the narrow space between gratitude expected and freedom denied. Kindness without freedom still demanded obedience, and obedience, however gently framed, remained captivity.

The Language He Chose

Language returned to him slowly and unevenly, shaped by years of enforced silence and the necessity of withholding speech for safety, so that words no longer came freely but waited to be tested before being released, and he understood far more than he allowed himself to say, remembering far more than he revealed. The household heard his accent before it grasped any meaning, listening to broken phrases and supplying their own conclusions, deciding in advance what he was capable of expressing and what lay beyond him, reading strain in his speech as limitation rather than caution. He did not correct this assumption, because correction required authority he did not possess, and misunderstanding, when it reduces scrutiny, becomes a form of shelter.

He chose his words with care, not to persuade or instruct but to endure, keeping sentences short, allowing errors to remain, accepting judgments about his speech because lowered expectations reduced pressure. A man thought simple is rarely pressed for explanation; a man assumed incapable of argument is seldom asked to defend himself. Outwardly, language diminished. Inwardly, it remained exact. The words he had learned in youth were not surrendered to time or neglect.

He carried the Divine Scripture as responsibility rather than ornament, preserved through memorization long before capture made books inaccessible, held line by line with precision shaped by discipline. It was not an isolated text but part of a continuum of revelation, demanding accuracy, sequence, and restraint, and he guarded it as one guards a trust. Each passage remained ordered in memory, rehearsed silently without embellishment, meaning preserved through repetition.

Image: 24 Qur'anic Invocation in Omar's Script Sacred words carried long before ink was allowed to receive them. What appears here was memorized when books were still possible, preserved when they were not.

Memory was active labor, not storage. What could not be spoken aloud was recited inwardly. What could not be written was traced mentally, verse following verse with care. This was not nostalgia or retreat into the past. It was maintenance. He understood that sacred words erode when neglected, losing clarity and force, becoming sentiment rather than command, and he refused that erosion even as his outward speech faltered and his accent was mistaken for ignorance. The structure of the

Divine Words remained intact within him, demanding and precise, shaping his inner hours when the outer ones belonged to others. In a household that believed authority resided in books it owned and laws it enforced, he carried a scripture that required neither shelf nor permission, ordering his inner life without announcement or display. He learned to use the language of the house instrumentally, answering commands, acknowledging questions, offering gratitude where expected, adopting their words without allowing those words to shape him. The language he chose was not the one that best expressed his interior life but the one that best protected it. This was not surrender but restraint refined by necessity.

Having lost the right to speak freely, he decided what speech was worth risk, resolving to speak only enough to remain intact and to allow underestimation if it preserved the deeper order he carried. Silence had preserved him before; controlled speech now served the same function. The household believed it was teaching him how to speak, but the truth was the opposite: he was deciding how much of himself would be heard, and in that quiet, deliberate decision he preserved continuity that ownership could not reach.

Chapter: 8 Faith in Captivity

Kindness can exist inside captivity without altering its truth.

Quote:

"I was treated gently, yet I remained owned."

What He Practiced

Faith did not leave him when freedom was taken; it adjusted its posture and continued under constraint. He lived among people who prayed differently, using words drawn from another lineage, another scripture, another history shaped by councils and crossings rather than memorization and chain transmission, yet when he listened to fragments carried through rooms or fields he recognized the underlying structure: praise before request, dependence acknowledged before desire, a turning toward the Creator rather than inward toward the self. This recognition mattered because it allowed him to remain intact without provoking attention or conflict. His faith did not require the rejection of theirs to survive, and he did not believe continuity was weakened by resemblance. He had learned long before capture that the Divine addresses peoples according to what seeps into their bones, and that shared form does not erase distinct command.

He practiced quietly, without announcement or display. The opening words he carried were few, complete, and sufficient: praise to the Lord of all existence, dependence declared without condition, a plea not for wealth, safety, or escape, but for guidance along a straight path. These words did not clash with what surrounded him and did not require correction or concealment through deception. They moved beneath the surface of daily life, parallel to what was spoken aloud, allowing him to remain aligned without drawing notice. When he heard the household's central prayers asking for daily provision, forgiveness, and protection from error, he did not resist or withdraw.

He recognized the same human posture standing exposed before higher authority, acknowledging need and limitation. This resemblance offered protection. It allowed his devotion to remain unseen rather than challenged.

Image: 25 Elderly man reading by lantern light The relationship endured because it had never depended on permission. What he practiced was not rebellion.

He did not perform rituals that would invite scrutiny or punishment. He did not argue theology he could not translate accurately into their language, knowing that partial explanation distorts rather than clarifies. He practiced alignment rather than instruction, intention rather than form, remembrance carried inwardly and sustained through consistency. Faith became something enacted without sound, maintained through repetition rather than declaration. Around him, many others were not afforded this narrow shelter. They came from lands shaped by their own inherited forms of devotion, carrying names for the Creator older than the soil they were now forced to work, and those forms were not tolerated as variation but targeted as threat.

Their practices were forbidden openly, treated as disorder rather than difference, replaced through force with prayers they did not recognize, punished when remembered aloud. For them, faith became dangerous even in private, because surveillance followed belief as closely as labor, and memory itself became a liability. He observed this without judgment and understood the cost clearly.

Survival, he learned, did not always depend on resistance, and resemblance could sometimes preserve what see-through opposition would destroy. He did not abandon what he had memorized. He did not dilute or revise it to fit expectation. He preserved it beneath the surface, practiced it without sound, allowed it to structure his inner hours while outwardly conforming to imposed routines.

This was not compromise of belief but continuity under restriction. Faith for him had never been performance, and it did not become so in captivity. It was fidelity expressed through care, precision, and restraint. The posture changed because the conditions demanded it, but the substance did not retreat.

Remembrance remained active, rehearsed deliberately, protected from erosion by neglect. In a world that attempted to regulate bodies, labor, and speech, remembrance proved more durable than any rule written to suppress it, because it did not require permission to exist and did not depend on visibility to endure.

What He Stopped Saying

There were words he did not lose and did not forget; he chose to withhold them, because speech had become a surface where meaning was altered the moment it appeared, bent by listeners trained to hear only compliance or difference, and he learned quickly that clarity invited correction while depth invited suspicion. He reduced his speech deliberately, not because language failed him but because it mattered too much to be spent where it would be misread or turned against him, and he stopped naming the obligations that ordered his days, stopped explaining the structure of his devotion, stopped correcting the assumptions made about him, allowing others to assign meaning to his silence and accepting the protection their misunderstanding provided.

There were names he no longer spoke aloud, not because they were forbidden by the Divine but because they had become dangerous among men, sacred words once pronounced openly now guarded like fire in dry conditions, carried without sound and repeated inwardly with the same precision they had once been given publicly.

He did not deny them and did not abandon them; he delayed them, understanding that timing had become as important as accuracy. He also stopped explaining resemblance and difference, no longer attempting to describe how the scripture he carried stood alongside the scripture they trusted, how the voices they revered and the words he preserved arose from the same source of command and mercy, because such explanation required a shared language that did not exist here, and without it truth would arrive not as illumination but as threat.

Image: 26 Qur'anic Invocation in Omar's Script Sacred words carried long before ink was allowed to receive them. What appears here was memorized when books were still possible, preserved when they were not.

He chose restraint over correction. This silence was not absence or retreat but discipline refined by circumstance, the practice of a man trained to guard language in environments hostile to meaning, speaking only when required, answering when addressed, offering gratitude when expected, while beneath these minimal exchanges a deeper language continued uninterrupted, shaping intention and ordering the inner hours with consistency.

He observed others forced into speech, men repeating words they did not recognize as their own to avoid punishment, devotion turned into performance through coercion, and he did not condemn them because he understood the calculation, that survival often demanded compliance and compliance often demanded spoken agreement. He chose another method, speaking less so that what remained unsaid could survive intact, allowing his voice to diminish outwardly so that his faith would not be reduced inwardly.

What he stopped saying did not fade or weaken; it accumulated weight, preserved through repetition without exposure, and in that silent accumulation he ensured that captivity would not determine which language governed his interior life.

Memory as Worship

What could no longer be practiced openly did not disappear but reorganized itself inwardly, and memory became the place where devotion was preserved intact, the last territory beyond inspection or command, treated not as refuge but as responsibility, because to remember correctly required care equal to any outward ritual.

Memory was not passive storage but active labor, requiring repetition, precision, and attention to order, sacred words recalled deliberately and without haste, not allowed to blur into sentiment, each passage revisited in its proper sequence, held long enough to confirm it had not shifted, then returned to its place, errors corrected when fatigue introduced them, pauses taken when exhaustion threatened accuracy, this steady work replacing what ritual once imposed by posture and time.

In this way memory became worship, not recollection for comfort but alignment maintained through effort, not a means of escape from surroundings but a method of remaining present within them without being reshaped by

them, allowing the scripture he carried to order his inner hours even when the outer ones were claimed by others, reminding him that time still answered to something

beyond ownership even when that answer could not be shown.

Image: 27 Portrait of Omar ibn Said This is the face of a man the country could not read. The eyes do not ask to be recognized. They endure. What he carried inwardly is not visible here, yet it governed his life more completely than anything taken from him.

He saw others remember differently, clinging to fragments without structure, melodies without context, names detached from meaning, memories that briefly comforted and then deepened loss, and he did not follow them into that drift, knowing that sacred memory loosened from form becomes longing rather than guidance.

He guarded against that erosion by preserving structure so meaning would not collapse under emotion. This labor was costly, demanding energy when energy was scarce, attention when attention might have been surrendered to fatigue, fidelity when the world offered only repetition without purpose, yet he persisted because abandoning memory would have allowed captivity to define the final shape of his inner life. No one witnessed this work, no one counted it as obedience or devotion, it produced no visible compliance and no visible resistance, existing entirely beyond the reach of command, and in that invisibility lay its strength, because memory could not be seized, sold, or legislated out of him.

In remembering, he did not retreat into the past but stood inside continuity, while the body aged, the language around him shifted, and the world he had known receded further each year, memory held its ground, preserving what had been entrusted to him not as relic but as living order. Worship continued without gesture, without sound, without permission, and in that quiet persistence he ensured that captivity could claim his labor, his movement, and his visibility, but not his allegiance.

Chapter: 9 Borrowed Time

Faith endures most clearly when it must survive without permission.

Quote:

"What is carried in memory cannot be confiscated."

The Body Weakens

Time no longer moved with him but over him, accumulating without ceremony and pressing into the body with a patience that outlasted resistance, and strength did not vanish suddenly but thinned in measurable ways, joints stiffening where response had once been immediate, breath shortening under labor previously endured without comment, the body that had survived road, sea, and pursuit now registering a different demand that arrived not as violence but as steady subtraction.

He did not complain, because complaint would have implied surprise and there was none; the body obeys time regardless of ownership, and what changed was not the presence of work but the cost of completing it. Tasks that once required endurance now required recovery, rest no longer restored what it had, and sleep fractured, shaped by waking pain rather than fear. He lived inside another man's time, and the days did not adjust for his weakening; the household rhythm remained fixed and indifferent, age granting no authority and instead increasing exposure, as slowness was noted, fatigue corrected, and limitation interpreted as failure rather than inevitability.

The obedience demanded of youth was required of age without modification or acknowledgment. He adapted quietly, making movement economical and rationing effort as carefully as food had once been rationed, learning where strength could still be spent and where it had to be withheld, the discipline that had shaped study now shaping survival, nothing wasted and nothing hurried, the body treated as a vessel still carrying something worth preserving even as its capacity diminished.

Pain became familiar and instructive, not sharp enough to alarm but constant enough to alter behavior, its contours learned through repetition, certain motions avoided, certain postures endured only briefly, limits communicated clearly by the body and respected because ignoring them would hasten collapse. Time belonged to others, seasons passing without altering expectation and years advancing without loosening claim, aging occurring not into rest but into continued use, and yet the weakening of the body did not confuse him about what had always been temporary.

Flesh had never been permanent, strength had never defined worth, and what changed was not identity but the care required to carry it. As physical power withdrew, he learned again what captivity could not fully control, because the order that had shaped him had never depended solely on muscle or endurance but on something quieter and more durable, something time could erode but not confiscate. He aged within another man's schedule, another man's demands, another man's indifference, carrying diminishing strength with the same restraint learned long before, and while the body weakened under years that did not belong to him, what governed him inwardly remained intact, continuing without permission, without display, and without surrender.

America Grows

The country changed while he remained fixed in place, expanding its boundaries outward while keeping his body confined within a narrow circle of obligation, roads extending, towns thickening, houses replacing fields, property changing hands, and laws multiplying without requiring his movement, all of it shaping the world that owned him.

He learned this change through fragments carried by others, references to conflicts and claims beyond his reach, to territories surveyed and settled, to harvests counted and markets widened, and he understood that none of it required his consent yet all of it depended on labor like his. The nation learned to speak in numbers, measuring itself constantly through acreage divided, yields recorded, populations tallied, and progress announced through accumulation rather than account, more land, more trade, more mouths sustained by systems that rendered certain labor invisible.

He observed this growth from within it, aware that the public celebration of expansion rested quietly on endurance that did not share in its reward. Time accelerated beyond him as new generations appeared, children born into a world that assumed its own permanence, speaking with assurance shaped by inheritance rather than necessity, the country imagining itself young even as it aged rapidly, its memory selective and its confidence unburdened by what it chose not to recall.

He remained where he was, because ownership does not require motion to exert control but continuity to maintain it, and he aged within a system that strengthened as his body weakened, the imbalance widening each year, his losses unrecovered as national milestones were marked and celebrated.

He heard scripture spoken openly and with confidence, rituals performed publicly and protected by law, faith permitted visibility and authority when aligned with power, and while he recognized familiar forms beneath different words, the distance grew as shared posture toward the Divine became wrapped in certainty that did not include him. His devotion endured without acknowledgment while others' devotion gained architecture, institutions, and permanence.

The country learned to name itself and to define freedom in terms that excluded him, to speak of destiny as possession rather than trust, and these words passed over him without invitation. He did not contest them, because contest requires standing and standing was not his condition, so he observed instead with attention sharpened by years of watching systems operate without explaining themselves.

He understood that expansion does not equal maturity, that accumulation does not guarantee wisdom, and that a nation can grow vast while remaining unacquainted with those whose labor carried its earliest weight. He watched confidence harden as memory narrowed, the country measuring progress forward while refusing backward account, and he recognized the contradiction not with bitterness but with clarity formed by endurance.

Image: 28 Westward expansion in rural America

As the years passed through events others named the war with Britain that confirmed independence, the steady westward push, the counting of people and property that made growth legible the structure around him became more assured of itself while his own position remained unchanged. He aged as the country advanced, the distance between those movements defining his life, the nation learning to imagine itself free while depending on unfreedom it refused to name.

He learned to survive within that contradiction, carrying memory forward in a place that preferred motion without remembrance, holding continuity where history hurried past it.

What grew around him did not recognize what remained within him, and yet both continued, bound together by time that belonged fully to neither, the country expanding into certainty while he persisted within constraint, his years accumulating quietly beneath a national story that moved loudly forward without pausing to look back.

Endurance

Endurance was not resistance and did not present itself as triumph or promise release; it functioned quietly, steadily, formed through long familiarity with limits that could not be crossed and obligations that could not be refused, living in daily decisions that preserved order even when disorder became permanent. He endured by accepting what could not be altered without allowing it to define him entirely, continuing to work as his body weakened, remaining useful enough to meet expectation while reserving what strength could not be replaced. Judgment mattered as much as patience, because excessive compliance hollowed the self while open defiance invited erasure, and he learned to live carefully within that narrow measure.

Years accumulated without distinction, seasons repeated, and faces around him changed as some disappeared and others arrived without knowledge of who he had been or how long he had already endured. He did not correct their assumptions, because correction required explanation and explanation required a world willing to listen, and endurance does not depend on recognition but on continuity. Faith did not soften with age; it sharpened inwardly, stripped of excess and reduced to what could not be compromised.

Memory remained active and exact, sacred words rehearsed silently not for comfort but for structure, ordering his inner life when the outer one belonged entirely to others and reminding him that endurance itself could become a form of obedience when obedience could no longer be seen.

He did not wait for freedom, because waiting assumes expectation and expectation invites disappointment, so he lived instead with acceptance refined into steadiness, each completed day sufficient and each act of remembrance enough.

Image: 29 End of the day in the fields

He measured success not by change in circumstance but by preservation of alignment. Endurance outlasts spectacle and does not seek witnesses or acknowledgment; it accumulates continuity rather than victory, and by the time age marked his body clearly, what he carried had already proven durable, having crossed ocean, road, fear, and time without dissolving. The world around him continued to change while he remained, not unchanged but unbroken, and though endurance did not restore what had been taken, it ensured that what remained could not be claimed by the same forces that had claimed everything else. In a life lived entirely within another man's time, endurance became the one measure that still belonged to him, and within that quiet, exacting measure he completed his days without surrendering the order that had first given them meaning.

Chapter: 10 Final Writing

A man can age inside another's time and still remain intact.

Quote:

"My strength weakened, but endurance remained."

Why He Writes

He writes because the body has begun to withdraw and silence alone will not carry what remains, because the hand that once moved with certainty now hesitates, the eyes no longer hold lines steady, and language that once obeyed precision arrives unevenly and resists recall, and he names this plainly without apology so the reader understands the condition under which these words are set down. He writes because memory, if kept only within him, will end when breath does, and this is not confession but custody transferred, a deliberate placing of sequence where weakness has begun to scatter it.

What he writes is not arranged for elegance or persuasion but for durability, ordered so it can outlast the body that carries it, because waiting for perfection would mean leaving nothing at all. He writes because others have spoken over him for most of his life, naming him without asking, interpreting restraint as simplicity and silence as absence, assigning meanings that served their comfort rather than his truth, and writing becomes the only remaining way to assert order without permission, to speak once without interruption, correction, or reduction.

He writes because faith requires witness rather than display, because what he carried inwardly for decades now seeks form not to argue doctrine but to testify to continuity, to show that the Words of the Divine did not leave him when practice became hidden or weaken when posture was denied, and writing becomes the final alignment the body can still perform, the last visible trace of an inward discipline that never surrendered.

Image: 30 Omar ibn Said's Manuscript in Archival Folder
Contained now within paper and frame, what was once
guarded only by memory rests in preservation. This folder
holds not a relic, but a witness—words carried across ocean
and time, finally permitted to remain.

He writes knowing the writing will be judged, anticipating readers unfamiliar with his references, a grammar marked by strain, a hand unsteady from age, and he meets this in humility rather than defense, offering acknowledgments not to disarm criticism but to clarify the cost of what is attempted. He writes because gratitude has not erased truth; he does not deny later kindness and names it carefully, but mercy does not cancel captivity and comfort does not rewrite origin, and writing allows both to exist without distortion or forced resolution.

He writes because time no longer offers delay, because the body signals clearly now as strength thins and breath shortens, and each line placed is an act completed before ability recedes further, done with restraint learned long ago, neither rushed nor postponed.

He writes because this is the final freedom left to him, not freedom of movement or choice, but freedom of order, the ability to say without interruption who he was before the breaking, during the breaking, and after it, what was taken, what remained, and what he guarded when everything else belonged to another.

He writes not to close his life but to place it where ownership cannot fully reach, fixing continuity on the page so that when the body can no longer carry it, the order he preserved will continue to speak.

What He Leaves Unsaid

There are matters he does not place on the page though he knows how to do so, not because they are forgotten but because they do not survive reduction without becoming something smaller and easier than they were, and a man trained in discipline understands that not everything entrusted to him is meant for display. He withholds the full measure of humiliation not because it was slight but because it was continuous, embedded in posture demanded without explanation, in correction delivered without limit, in the daily management of a body whose consent was assumed, and to catalogue it would require dwelling there again and turning the act of writing into another enclosure.

He withholds the details of violence not to spare the reader but to preserve proportion, because pain, when itemized, invites spectacle and diverts attention from what mattered most, which was not the form of harm but its purpose, the attempted erasure of order and continuity, an attempt that did not succeed. He withholds bitterness not because it was unavailable but because it would have been effortless to cultivate, and ease has never been his measure; bitterness grows readily where injustice persists, but the page is not offered as a vessel for grievance, and he declines to let resentment determine the shape of his record.

He withholds the hours when faith strained under exhaustion and fear, when memory required effort rather than ease and silence weighed heavily, not because faith was untested but because doubt did not govern the outcome, and to dramatize those hours would grant them authority they did not retain.

He withholds names beyond what clarifies structure, not because those who wronged him were insignificant but because naming grants permanence, and he has watched systems preserve themselves by recording what serves them; he will not do the same for cruelty by immortalizing it. What remains unsaid is not absence but restraint, the shaping pressure around what he does choose to give, defining weight through omission rather than accumulation. Silence here is not evasion but judgment exercised deliberately, a final application of the discipline that governed his life, deciding what could be spoken without distortion and what had to be carried without witness. He understands readers will imagine what is missing and allows that, because meaning does not require total exposure but integrity, and integrity requires proportion.

He gives what must be given to establish continuity and withholds what would diminish truth by turning it into consumption. In leaving certain things unsaid he preserves the order he guarded across years of confinement and misreading, ensuring that the record does not become another instrument of control or spectacle, and that preservation, intact to the end, stands as the most accurate testimony he can offer.

Ink as Witness

There are matters he does not place on the page though he knows how to do so, not because they are forgotten but because they do not survive reduction without becoming something smaller and easier than they were, and a man trained in discipline understands that not everything entrusted to him is meant for display. He withholds the full measure of humiliation not because it was slight but because it was continuous, embedded in posture demanded without explanation, in correction delivered without limit, in the daily management of a body whose consent was assumed, and to catalogue it would require dwelling there again and turning the act of writing into another enclosure.

He withholds the details of violence not to spare the reader but to preserve proportion, because pain, when itemized, invites spectacle and diverts attention from what mattered most, which was not the form of harm but its purpose, the attempted erasure of order and continuity, an attempt that did not succeed. He withholds bitterness not because it was unavailable but because it would have been effortless to cultivate, and ease has never been his measure; bitterness grows readily where injustice persists, but the page is not offered as a vessel for grievance, and he declines to let resentment determine the shape of his record.

He withholds the hours when faith strained under exhaustion and fear, when memory required effort rather than ease and silence weighed heavily, not because faith was untested but because doubt did not govern the outcome, and to dramatize those hours would grant them authority they did not retain.

He withholds names beyond what clarifies structure, not because those who wronged him were insignificant but because naming grants permanence, and he has watched systems preserve themselves by recording what serves them; he will not do the same for cruelty by immortalizing it.

What remains unsaid is not absence but restraint, the shaping pressure around what he does choose to give, defining weight through omission rather than accumulation. Silence here is not evasion but judgment exercised deliberately, a final application of the discipline that governed his life, deciding what could be spoken without distortion and what had to be carried without witness. He understands readers will imagine what is missing and allows that, because meaning does not require total exposure but integrity, and integrity requires proportion.

He gives what must be given to establish continuity and withholds what would diminish truth by turning it into consumption. In leaving certain things unsaid he preserves the order he guarded across years of confinement and misreading, ensuring that the record does not become another instrument of control or spectacle, and that preservation, intact to the end, stands as the most accurate testimony he can offer.

This record ends where the hand could no longer continue.

Image: 31 A modern historical marker identifying Omar ibn Said, erected long after his death.

Timeline

Born, Futa Toro (present-day Senegal), ca. 1770

Captured and sold into the trans-Atlantic slave trade, 1807

Middle Passage to Charleston, South Carolina, 1807–1808

Escape and capture in Fayetteville, North Carolina, ca. 1810

Arabic manuscript written, 1831

Death in North Carolina, ca. 1863–1864

Sources & Acknowledgments

This book is anchored in the surviving Arabic manuscript written by Omar ibn Said in the final years of his life, preserved in the collections of the Library of Congress. That document remains the primary witness to his own voice, faith, and restraint, and it has governed both the tone and the limits of this work.

Historical context has been informed by established research on the Senegal River region of West Africa, particularly Futa Toro, and its traditions of sacred learning in the eighteenth century. Contextual understanding of the transatlantic slave trade, the Middle Passage, and early nineteenth-century enslavement in Charleston and North Carolina has guided the narrative framework within which Omar ibn Said's life unfolded.

Existing translations and studies of Omar ibn Said's manuscript, along with broader scholarship on enslaved African Muslims in the Americas, have been consulted where they clarify practice, environment, and chronology. These sources are treated as support rather than authority, serving the record rather than reshaping it.
Gratitude is owed to the unnamed lives that appear only briefly in archives, and to the many whose faith and endurance were never recorded at all. Their absence is part of the history this book carries.
Any errors of interpretation or emphasis belong to the author alone.

nationalhumanitiescenter.org
Wikipedia
NCPedia
nationalhumanitiescenter.org
NC DNCR

Image Credits

Manuscript images and Arabic writings attributed to Omar ibn Said are reproduced from public-domain holdings of the Library of Congress. These materials are presented for historical reference and contextual accuracy. No alterations have been made beyond sizing and tonal adjustment for print clarity.

HISTORICAL SOURCES (PUBLIC DOMAIN)

Image 1
Riding through the savanna on a donkey.
Illustrative historical scene representing travel and daily life in West Africa prior to capture. Public domain reference image.

Image 2
Omar ibn Said's Handwriting (Opening Page).
Arabic manuscript page written by Omar ibn Said. Library of Congress. Public domain.

Image 3
Islamic school in Senegal's evening light.
Illustrative reference depicting Qur'anic instruction and scholarly training in West Africa. Public domain reference image.

Image 4
Manuscript Page with Autobiographical Lines.
Original Arabic manuscript page written by Omar ibn Said, recording education, capture, and removal. Library of Congress. Public domain.

Image 5
European raiders assault West African village.
Nineteenth-century engraving depicting armed raids and
village destruction during slave capture. Public domain.

Image 6
Manuscript Page with Autobiographical Lines.
Additional Arabic manuscript page by Omar ibn Said.
Library of Congress. Public domain.

Image 7
Burning of a Village in Africa and Capture of Its Inhabitants.
Illustrated report depicting forced capture through
destruction, February 1859. Public domain.

Image 9
Qur'anic Passages Written in Captivity.
Arabic religious text written by Omar ibn Said while
enslaved. Library of Congress. Public domain.

Image 10
The Africans of the Slave Bark *Wildfire*.
Nineteenth-century illustration documenting the
conditions of captives aboard a slave ship. Public domain.

Image 11
Slave Ship Interior Diagram.
Abolitionist-era diagram illustrating spatial arrangement
and confinement aboard a trans-Atlantic slave vessel.
Public domain.

Image 12
Storm at sea: shipwreck and chaos.
Nineteenth-century maritime illustration representing
storms and peril during Atlantic crossings. Public domain.

Image 13
Arrival and Sale.
Nineteenth-century engraving depicting inspection and sale of captives upon arrival in the Americas. Public domain.

Image 14
Inspection and Sale of an Enslaved Person.
Nineteenth-century engraving commonly titled "Inspection and Sale of a Negro." Public domain.

Image 19
Qur'anic Invocation in Omar's Script.
Arabic invocation written by Omar ibn Said. Library of Congress. Public domain.

Image 21
Qur'anic Invocation in Omar's Script.
Additional Arabic manuscript page written by Omar ibn Said. Library of Congress. Public domain.

Image 31
Omar ibn Said Historical Marker, Bladen County, North Carolina.
Photograph of a modern roadside historical marker erected long after his death. Used for historical reference.

ORIGINAL ILLUSTRATIONS (AI-GENERATED FOR THIS PUBLICATION)

The following illustrations were created specifically for this book to support narrative visualization where no historical image exists. These images are interpretive and not documentary.

Image 3 (AI)
A Life Shaped by Discipline.
Original illustration depicting Islamic learning in West
Africa with wooden tablets.

Image 4 (AI)
The Day Order Collapsed.
Original historical scene depicting the violent raid and
capture of an African village.

Image 6 (AI)
The Road to the Great Water.
Original illustration depicting forced marches toward the
coast.

Image 12 (AI)
Bodies, Time, Silence.
Original maritime scene depicting storm and chaos at sea.

Image 13 (AI)
Arrival Without Arrival.
Original illustration depicting the unloading and inspection
of captives at port.

Image 15 (AI)
Hunger, Distance, Prayer.
Original illustration depicting flight, exhaustion, and inward
prayer during escape.

Image 18 (AI)
Clean Clothes, Unclean Truth.
Original interior scene depicting imposed civility masking
captivity.

Image 20 (AI)
What He Practiced.
Original illustration depicting private remembrance and inward devotion.

Image 22 (AI)
America Grows.
Original landscape illustration depicting national expansion alongside enslavement.

Image 24 (AI)
Endurance.
Original portrait-style illustration depicting aging, restraint, and survival.

Book Cover Illustration (AI)
Original cover artwork depicting Omar ibn Said seated outside a rural American structure, created for this publication.

115